LIFE & LETTERS

Alan Powers

LIFE & LETTERS
THE SPECTATOR COLUMNS

ALLAN MASSIE

QUARTET

First published in 2013 by Quartet Books Limited
A member of the Namara Group
27 Goodge Street, London W1T 2LD
Copyright © Allan Massie 2013
The right of Allan Massie to be identified
as the author of this work has been asserted
by him in accordance with the
Copyright, Designs and Patents Act, 1988

A catalogue record for this book
is available from the British Library
ISBN 978 0 7043 7265 8
Typeset by Josh Bryson
Printed and bound in Great Britain by
T J International Ltd, Padstow, Cornwall

For Robert Nye

CONTENTS

THE FATE OF THE
RUNNING MAN

20 MAY 2006

Evelyn Waugh told Ann Fleming that 'Tony Powell's latest volume [*Casanova's Chinese Restaurant*] is a sad disappointment — only three pages of Widmerpool'. That was in 1960. A few years earlier, my classics master, urging me to read Powell, said, 'The pre-war novels; I don't like this chap Widmerpool.' Few Powell fans would agree. Most are on Waugh's side, delighting in the monster.

Still, I've been thinking about a question posed by Colin Donald in a paper given at last December's Anthony Powell Centenary Conference. 'Does Widmerpool "add up" as a character?' he asked. 'He certainly has a varied career, progressing from awkward, unpopular boy to crazed, elderly hippy via stints as a solicitor's clerk, bill broker, territorial officer, wartime major and DAAG, Cabinet Office military martinet, Labour MP, publisher, suspected Russian agent, university teacher, TV personality, Californian guru, trendy university chancellor and spectacularly embarrassing cult member' — a list which omits only his time on Sir Magnus Donners' staff.

A varied career, certainly, not necessarily an incredible one. A reading from the volume entitled *Eccentrics* in the collection of *Daily Telegraph* obituaries yields comparable examples of wayward lives. The question is whether we believe in Widmerpool right up to his last metamorphosis as a seeker of 'harmony' in Scorp Mortlock's cult?

There is another pertinent question. How much of Widmerpool's career did Powell foresee when he introduced us to this figure 'in a sweater once white and cap at least a size too small, on the flat heels of spiked running shoes'? Not necessarily a great deal. It's unlikely that he knew then that Widmerpool would die shouting, 'I'm running, I'm running, I've got to keep it up.'

For one thing, Powell told me he didn't do 'a lot of overall planning'. In this context he remarked that when Stringham says of Widmerpool 'that boy will be the death of me', he didn't then know that Widmerpool would indeed be responsible for sending Stringham to Singapore where he died in a Japanese PoW camp. Stringham's quip, which was 'the sort of thing people said then', was a happy chance.

One of the problems of *Dance*, read as a coherent work, is that Powell started writing it years before the time in which the last two books are set. Accordingly, though Jenkins is in a sense remembering the story, he starts telling it long before it is completed. In writing a novel over a period of 25 years, Powell responded to changes in what was acceptable, being aware also that, unavoidably, he himself changed too. Pamela Flitton, for instance, would have had to be treated differently but for the greater freedom granted a novelist in the post-Chatterley trial mood of the Sixties, though he did not doubt his ability 'to have attacked her in a more roundabout way'.

This suggests that had Powell published a novel every year rather than biennially, bringing out the last volume in 1963 rather than 1975, Widmerpool's end would have been different, perhaps less awful. His disintegration, recorded with appalling zest in the last two books, could not have taken just the same form before the Sixties.

Nevertheless, though Widmerpool's final appearance as that 'spectacularly embarrassing cult member' is far removed from the stolid, awkward schoolboy we first encountered, the seed was indeed planted early, even if Powell himself did not know how it would grow. When Jenkins meets him at La Grenadière after leaving school he still thinks of him as 'an ineffective person, rather a freak'; yet the reader is already aware of his strength of will and determination to excel — even if Jenkins thinks his expressed ambition to be 'such rubbish that I changed the subject'.

It is Widmerpool's determination to live by the will, to impose himself on others, insensitive to their feelings, indifferent to anything but his own interest, which gives unity to his life, making him, for all his erratic course, 'add up' as a character. Without imagination, in thrall to the ego, the failure of his respectable career brings this once so conventional boy (shocked to learn that Peter Templar 'had a woman before he left' Eton) to the point where he rejects 'all bourgeois values'. There is nowhere else left for him to go.

A LATE BEGINNER

3 JUNE 2006

Sometimes at book festivals I am asked which historical novelists I most admire and enjoy. 'Alfred Duggan,' I say first, and am usually met with a blank response. This is not entirely surprising. Duggan died in 1964 and most of his books are out of print.

Some will know of him as a friend of Evelyn Waugh from Oxford days. 'A full-blooded rake ... we were often drunk ... Alfred almost always.' He remained in this condition for some 20 years, Waugh himself eventually doing much to rescue him from alcoholism. So there was an unusual pattern to his career, as Waugh remarked in an article published in *The Spectator* soon after his friend's death. 'In recent years we have become so familiar with the spectacle of personal frustration and disaster in the artistic life that we have come to regard it as normal.' He cited Scott Fitzgerald and Dylan Thomas as examples of writers 'who began with early brilliance and popular recognition, only to find in early middle age that their powers were exhausted and that nothing remained for them except self-pity and drunkenness'. He might have added Hemingway to the list.

Alfred Duggan's case was the reverse. Drunk and dissolute for years, he seemed like a man doomed to waste his life. Then he gave up drink, was received into the Catholic church, set himself to write, and published the first of his 15 novels, *Knight with Armour*, in 1950.

That first novel was about the Crusades; so was his last, *Count Bohemund*. Between them he ranged over the Roman empire, the Dark Ages and early mediaeval times. None of the books is set later than the thirteenth century. According to Waugh, he said, with 'less than candour', that he chose to restrict himself to these periods because the scantiness of the sources relieved him of the labour of research. If there was any truth in this remark, it showed that he was possessed of a fine artistic sense. Research can so easily smother a novel. More to the point, by confining himself to these centuries he found a solution to the most taxing problem that confronts a writer of historical fiction: how best to render the speech of your characters. None of Duggan's spoke English. Therefore he was free to have them speak in the language of his own time. It was as if he was translating their words and thoughts into modern speech.

Yet the real reason for his choice of period and setting was that he felt at home there. He had read widely for years, even in his drinking days, and had travelled extensively in Europe and the Levant. He was soaked in his material, and it had been long maturing. This accounts for what Waugh identified as 'the sense of intimacy' which the novels offer. It is 'as though he were describing personal experiences and observation'.

There is in the novels that unmistakable ring of authority and authenticity. This is the case, whether they are written in the first person or the third. He employed both with equal felicity, and it is impossible to decide why he selected one mode for a particular novel, the other for another.

The narrative style is generally deadpan, without flourishes, though laced with irony. *Family Favourites* begins, 'You may think it odd that a mere Praetorian can write easily enough to compose his memoirs; in general we are a rough lot.' Utterly convincing, and a splendidly flat introduction to the story of the teenage Elagabalus, blond beauty (and god) equally devoted to his esoteric religion and to stable-boys. The book is very funny and strangely moving.

The acuteness and depth of Duggan's historical imagination allow him time and again to hit on a revealing moment. *The Conscience of the King*, for instance, tells the story of Cerdic. He is a Romanised Briton who becomes, by a series of quite probable accidents, the leader of a Saxon war-band and then founder of the Wessex kingdom. The turning point of his life comes one afternoon in August: 'I was sitting in the courtyard behind my father's house, basking in the sun and reading the poems of Ovid (now I come to think of it, that was the last occasion I read a book).' In that casual parenthesis Duggan illuminates for us the passage of Roman civilisation to the barbarian world. And how appropriate his choice of Ovid, elegant and artificial poet of love, author also of *Metamorphoses*, as Cerdic's last read. Duggan brings off such strokes time and again.

KEEPING THE BALANCE
17 JUNE 2006

In a volume of his posthumously published notebooks (*Garder Tout en Composant Tout*), Henry de Montherlant remarks: '*Je ne sais pourquoi nous faisons des descriptions, puisque le lecteur ne les lit jamais.*' Well said, but not quite true; there are readers who dote on long descriptive passages. Alain de Botton for instance wrote recently that the best bits of Proust are the descriptions and passages of analysis. Yet for me these are just the parts of *À la Recherche* which seem stale, while the characters and conversation remain entrancing.

So I find myself on Montherlant's side. Devoted though I am to the Waverley novels, my eyes tend to glaze on coming upon long paragraphs describing mountain scenery or the dress and armour of a mediaeval knight, and I resort to what Scott himself called 'the laudable practice of skipping'.

We are in good company. 'Damn description, it is always disgusting,' said Byron, though no mean hand at it himself. 'Description is always a bore,' was Disraeli's dandyish view. More surprisingly perhaps, Stevenson observed that 'no human being ever spoke of scenery for above two minutes, which makes me suspect we hear too much of it in literature'. Yet it's a rare novel that dispenses entirely with it, though Ivy Compton-Burnett's come close to doing so. 'I don't know if you care for descriptions?' she asked the novelist Elizabeth Taylor, adding, 'I don't.'

Description used to be all the thing. In *Cakes and Ale* Maugham tells us that the 'prime' of his Grand Old Man of English letters, Edward Driffield:

belonged to the period when the purple patch was in vogue, and there are descriptive passages in his works that have found their way into all the anthologies of English prose. His pieces on the sea and spring in the Kentish woods and sunset on the lower reaches of the Thames are famous. It should be a mortification to me that I cannot read them without discomfort.

Nevertheless Maugham himself, like Edmund Wilson and Scott Fitzgerald, sprinkled his notebooks with descriptive paragraphs, some decidedly purple. I wonder when he thought he would use them.

It seems to me that description has three functions in a novel. First, obviously it allows the reader to picture the scene. This is best done briefly. The longer the description, the more difficult for the reader to form an image; he is swamped by detail. A few lines make a picture:

> The hills across the valley of the Ebro were long and white. On this side there was no shade and no trees and the station was between two lines of rails in the sun. Close against the side of the station there was the warm shadow of the building and a curtain, made of strings of bamboo beads, hung across the open door into the bar, to keep out flies.

Hemingway is the master of this sort of thing, and casts a longer shadow than the wall of that building; the problem for writers even now is to avoid sounding like a faint echo.

Second, description creates mood. Here one might quote Hemingway again or Simenon or Graham Greene, all of whom use description so exactly and economically that mood and picture become as one. A good example of this is offered by the first page of *The Honorary Consul*, too long to quote here; it establishes the tone of the novel.

Third, a writer may use passages of description to modulate the pace of his novel. Action, dialogue, reflection (or analysis), description: these are the elements of a work of fiction; and the success of a novel may depend to an extent of which the reader is not consciously aware, but which he yet feels or senses, on the ability of the author to achieve a satisfying balance between them. The objection Montherlant voiced — with which I sympathise — is really valid only when that balance has not been realised, and when long descriptive passages weigh down and retard the narrative, directing the reader's attention (if he doesn't choose to skip) to the author's way with words, rather than allowing these passages to contribute to the narrative flow.

THE ART OF THE IRRELEVANT

1 JULY 2006

Asked whether a good review would sell a book, the publisher Rupert Hart-Davies replied, 'No, but a concatenation of good ones may do so.' One would like to think this true, even while observing that the bestseller lists regularly feature novels which are either not reviewed at all, or have been given brief and sometimes scornful notices. No doubt this was always the case, sales of the likes of Edgar Wallace and Dennis Wheatley not depending on reviews. The means by which a book becomes a bestseller have always been mysterious, though nowadays the level of the promotion budget and the willingness of publishers to pay for lavish displays in bookshops seem also essential to the creation of a bestseller.

Few literary novels come into that category. Therefore one might expect reviews to play a bigger part in determining their sales. Certainly publishers remain eager to secure reviews, though not, I suspect, half as anxious as the author, for whom a review may be the only evidence that anyone has actually read his book. But what difference does it make? More than 20 years ago, when Auberon Waugh wrote a full-page weekly review in the *Evening Standard*, he modestly suggested to me that his recommendation might be worth at most 200 additional sales. Given that the paper must then have had more than a million readers, this is not an impressive figure; but I doubt if any other reviewer could honestly have claimed to have had even that much influence. I have reviewed new novels in *The Scotsman* for 30 years now, and in that time not more than a dozen readers have ever thanked me for introducing them to the work of a particular writer.

Many novelists will have had the experience of receiving glowing reviews — even a concatenation of them — only to find, months later, that the enthusiasm of reviewers has not been reflected in sales. They then, quite naturally, are likely to blame their publisher, asking why he hasn't promoted the book vigorously on the strength of this chorus of praise. Brief reflection or self-examination on the part of the disgruntled author might be chastening. How often, he might ask himself, has he bought a book because of a review?

Still, it is better to be reviewed than not to be reviewed, since at the very least a review offers publisher and author free publicity. A literary novel or biography that gets no reviews drops into a black hole, though these days the author may have recourse to the internet to try to call attention to his work.

Why do people read reviews if not to decide if they want to buy the book being reviewed? The short answer is that they do so for the same reasons that they read other parts of the newspaper or magazine: for information, for entertainment, and for enlightenment.

Information: people of a certain level of culture like to know what is being published, which authors are up and which down, what sort of questions are being addressed, and so on. The desire to be well-informed is natural to us, and people with an interest in literature read book reviews as those with an interest in cricket or football read the sports pages.

Entertainment: a good reviewer is a craftsman, each review a little essay intended to give pleasure by the manner in which it is written as well as by the interest in the book under review. The reviewer is a sort of columnist, and like the columnist must arrange his material in such a way as to please the reader. Otherwise he will not be read. Incidentally, it is much harder to write an entertaining review of a novel — unless it is a bad one — than of, say, a biography.

Enlightenment: this may seem to be claiming too much for mere book reviews. Yet, like many, I owe much of my early literary education to reviewers such as Cyril Connolly, John Davenport and Philip Toynbee. Reading them every week in the *Sunday Times* or the *Observer* contributed to the formation of taste and developed an understanding of how what was being written then related to what had been written in the past. V. S. Pritchett, Anthony Powell and Rebecca West were other reviewers whose articles were educational as well as enjoyable.

PRINCE OF SELF-PITY

15 JULY 2006

T. S. Eliot thought *Hamlet* an 'artistic failure', Shakespeare being unable to reconcile the theme of the old revenge tragedy on which the work is based with the conception of the character of Hamlet himself. One may agree with this while still finding the play compelling; indeed the most puzzling of the tragedies.

The revenge theme is admittedly tiresome and the reasons for postponing the act of vengeance both unconvincing and boring. We can accept the ghost only as a convenient theatrical convention. No doubt Elizabethan audiences saw it differently. Belief in ghosts was then common, and one wonders to what extent Shakespeare shared it. Banquo's ghost appears only to Macbeth and is invisible to the other dinner-guests; invisible to Lady Macbeth also. So the ghost scene in that play is psychologically convincing. It's different in *Hamlet*. Francisco, Bernardo and Horatio all see the ghost, though it refuses to speak to them; subsequently speaking only to Hamlet himself. This suggests that Shakespeare may have regarded the ghost as something more than a useful dramatic device. But it is the character of Hamlet that gives the play its perennial interest, and it is his character which puzzles us, or ought to do so.

Is he a good man? Paul Johnson in a recent essay calls him a 'paragon' and a 'confused but essentially benevolent young genius'. Considering what a botch he makes of things, 'genius' seems an overstatement. An earlier Johnson (Samuel) thought he was 'represented as a virtuous character', but clearly had doubts, being shocked, as a Christian, by the speech in which Hamlet resolves not to kill the king while he is at prayer, preferring to wait till he is 'at some act/That has no relish of salvation in't.' Johnson found this speech 'in which Hamlet... is not content with taking blood for blood, but contrives damnation for the man he would punish, too horrible to be read or to be uttered'.

Hamlet can be played as an indecisive and self-questioning Romantic intellectual (the Gielgud interpretation), or as a mixed-up kid, immature, uncertain of himself, veering from self-love to self-loathing by way of self-pity. His obsession with his mother — unhealthy and quasi-incestuous, as Olivier played it — marks him off from Osborne's Jimmy Porter, the quintessential 1950s Angry Young Man.

Yet Hamlet, if emotionally immature, isn't a boy. On the evidence of the gravediggers' scene, he is 30. This prompted Auden to ask why he is still a student. (Doing a PhD at Wittenberg, perhaps?) It makes me wonder why everyone seems to have accepted without demur that Claudius should succeed his brother as king, rather than the Prince who is heir-apparent. This is all the stranger because Claudius tells us that Hamlet 'is lov'd of the distracted multitude' — like Edward VIII? Did the Establishment, as in Edward's case, see something unstable and rotten in him?

If so, they had a point, for when we look at what Hamlet does, rather than losing ourselves in admiration of his words, he seems more villainous than virtuous. He hesitates to kill the king, but murders Polonius, and shows no remorse — 'Thou wretched, rash, intruding fool, farewell.' He arranges the murder of Rosencrantz and Guildenstern, and then boasts to Horatio of his cleverness in doing so; not very nice. He is brutal to Ophelia and also to the Queen — the 'rank, sweat of an enseamed bed,/Stew'd in corruption' speech is disgusting: no way to speak to your mother. He is also a hypocrite, boasting of his love for Ophelia after he had driven her to madness and suicide; and while he piously turns away from suicide himself because 'the Everlasting hath set his canon 'gainst self-slaughter', the divine prohibition of murder does not appear to trouble him.

Of course, he is attractive, witty, with a smart line in repartee: a 'prince of gestures', as Peter Vansittart has called him. But Shakespeare knew that villains are often capable of exercising great charm. Think of Richard III, Edmund, even Iago. Finally, Hamlet is full of self-pity: 'The time is out of joint; O cursed spite,/That ever I was born to set it right.' Self-pity is unattractive in real life; not necessarily so in literature. Indeed, Anthony Powell thought 'immense self-pity an almost essential adjunct of the bestseller'. Hamlet has self-pity in spades, and it is perhaps this, as much as anything, which accounts for his appeal and popularity.

SNOW ON THE WAY AGAIN?

29 JULY 2006

Anthony Powell's centenary last year was rightly celebrated; not much notice, I think, was taken of C. P. Snow's. This was hardly surprising. Shares in *Snow Preferred* are, in Wodehouse's phrase, 'down in the cellar with no takers'. I would guess that very few under the age of, say, 50 have read the 11 volumes of his *Strangers and Brothers* sequence, published between 1940 and 1970. Yet he was then regarded as a major English novelist, and the sequence as being as important and ambitious as Powell's.

Malcolm Bradbury, who had, I suspect, as a young man a greater admiration for Snow's work than when he came to write *The Modern English Novel* (1993), described the sequence as:

> Modern history seen from the inside, an account of the intentions and conflicts of the teachers, academics, lawyers, politicians, scientists and bureaucrats who over the troubled and often anarchic march of history hope to make reason, justice and progress prevail in human affairs, and who eventually shape and administer the changes in postwar Britain.

This is a fair enough summary, though it makes the novels seem more arid than they are. But at least it makes it clear that Snow had a real and worthwhile subject matter, something that can't be said of all admired novelists today. He wrote for grown-ups and he is one of the few English novelists capable of writing seriously and intelligently about public life, about men — rarely women — who get things done.

16

SNOW ON THE WAY AGAIN?

There's a passage in *Homecomings*, one of the best novels in the sequence, which admirably displays his understanding of these matters. His narrator, Lewis Eliot, a lawyer, is a wartime civil servant; the head of his department, Hector Rose, is a man with an 'aptitude for power':

> Since the war began he had been totally immersed in it, carrying responsibility without a blink. It was a lesson to me, I sometimes thought, about how wrong one can be. For, in the great political divide before the war, it was not only Lufkin's business associates who were on the opposite side to me. Bevill, the old aristocratic handyman of a politician, had been a Municheer; so had Rose and other up-and- coming civil servants. I had not known Rose then; if I had done I should have distrusted him when it came to a crisis. I should have been dead wrong. Actually when war came Bevill and Rose were as wholehearted as men could be. Compared with my friends on the irregular Left, their nerves were stronger.

That passage shows many of Snow's strengths: his lucidity, his fairness, his grasp of character, his understanding of both the nature and demands of public life. He is capable of dealing with big subjects: *The New Men*, for example, is concerned with the moral and political questions arising from the project to develop the atom bomb. He knows the importance of work to his characters. You feel that his businessmen might really be capable of running a business and his civil servants of managing a department.

His weaknesses are equally apparent. His power of invention was poor. Though he sometimes brings off brief and effective snatches of scene-setting, there is no poetry in him and, worse for a novelist, precious little humour. (Powell, recalling a trip to a writers' conference in Bulgaria, thought he 'conveyed the impression of having emerged from the pages of one of his own works . . . he did not himself deal in jokes, but had no objection to them). When he attempts a comic character — the aged don M. H. L. Gay in *The Masters*, for instance — he is not successful. Then his seriousness can drift into solemnity, pomposity even. His prose has a machine-made ring. The understanding of character sometimes dwindles into a man-of-affairs knowingness, judgments too easy, glib, unearned. As against that, he is good on frustration, disappointment, envy, resentment.

He doesn't deserve his present neglect. Certainly the work is dated. He wrote of academics before they were thrust into the market-place, of civil servants confident in their ability to manage the affairs of the nation and not yet beset by the whims and follies of management consultants. The 'corridors of power' — title of one of the novels, but already used in an earlier one — ring differently now. In his time he was compared to Trollope, and it may be that his posthumous reputation will be like Trollope's too: a period of neglect, when his work was despised or disparaged by a more self-conscious generation of novelists and critics, followed by a return to favour, that return being led by the Common Reader.

FATAL ATTRACTION

12 AUGUST 2006

When Prince Harry stirred up a fuss by wearing Nazi uniform to a fancy-dress party he found a gallant defender in Paul Johnson who wrote that 'in treating Nazi insignia as a party joke' the young prince 'reflects the instincts of his generation'. 'The Nazis,' he added, 'do have an undoubted fascination for many young people', because of their style, not their ideology. 'Hitler still exerts some of the dread appeal he exercised in his lifetime ... A lot of his appeal, I suspect, is visual. Hitler was a kind of artist' who 'put his artistic and inventive instincts to work'.

This is surely undeniable, and Johnson is by no means the first to remark it. Thomas Mann was there before him. In 1938, by then exiled from Germany, he wrote an essay entitled *Brother Hitler*. 'The fellow is a catastrophe; that is no reason to find him uninteresting as character and destiny,' he loftily declared. But what sort of interest? The essay's title is significant. Mann, the great novelist, the correct bourgeois family man, pillar of public rectitude, recognises his kinship with the catastrophic fellow, with 'this unqualified, impossible man . . . this rejected Bohemian artist'.

Rejected indeed, failing even to gain admittance to the Vienna Academy of Arts, getting no further than peddling his little postcards round the coffee houses. In contrast, Mann's success came early; he was only 25 when *Buddenbrooks* was published. And yet in his eyes they are brothers. He himself was not only the respectable son of the Lübeck patriciate; he was also the artist whose inclination was towards homo-eroticism which he associated with aesthetics and death. 'That all artistic genius inclines in that direction, tends towards the abyss is all too certain,' he wrote.

There was an element in him which identified with the Bohemian failure. Why not? The finest novel is an imperfect realisation of what the author envisaged. He saw in Hitler the type of the unsuccessful artist, the layabout — what, had the wheel turned differently, he might have been himself: 'basically arrogant, with his basically I'm-too-good-for-that rejection of any rational and reputable activity.' And what was the basis of this? Why, the artist's assumption that he was reserved for something special, 'entirely indefinable'. He recognised in Hitler, and in himself, 'the dream of seeing a world lost in fear, love, admiration, shame, at the feet of the once-spurned man' — the dream of nights in the garret or doss-house.

Hitler is first the rejected artist, always believing himself misunderstood, therefore full of resentment. The type is common. But he finds another art he can excel in: the art of rhetoric. Yet even in power the artist-Führer, like the successful novelist Mann, can never be satisfied. There is still 'the insatiability of the drive for compensation and self-glorification'; also 'the feeling of futility as soon as there is nothing to do' — the novel finished, the great speech made — and then there is 'the insomniac force of always having to prove oneself again'. Mann's biographer, Hermann Kurzke, writes, 'The will to power gives impetus to the practice of art as it does to politics.'

'There is a lot of "Hitler" in Wagner,' Mann wrote (after the war). Not 'Wagner' in Hitler; that's commonplace, but 'Hitler' in Wagner: a much keener observation. What is it that he sees? The determination to go beyond what has been achieved before? Perhaps. What Matthew Arnold called 'Titanism'? That too, I should say. But also Mann observed that for Hitler 'to stand Wagner-like, on the doorstep of ruination, is everything'. And he wrote that in

1938 before the Nazis' own *Götterdämmerung*. Mann recognised in this catastrophic brother the magnetic attraction towards disaster. Borges saw it too, remarking on the 'unreality' of Nazism, on the will to destruction, since nobody, not even Hitler, he thought, 'in the intimacy of his soul' truly wishes Hell to triumph.

Yet Hell has its sinister glamour, for the Romantic artist as for adolescents. Mann knew this, explored it in *Dr Faustus*, his profound, disturbing reflection on the German catastrophe. 'It is precisely Hitler's gifts,' Paul Johnson wrote, 'which make him so dangerous and so uniquely evil.' The fellow was a catastrophe undoubtedly. What would he have been if the Vienna Academy had accepted and trained him and he had made a living as a second-rate landscape painter? Cream-cake-eating darling of a coterie of ladies in a provincial town? Perhaps.

THE WISDOM OF
SANDY ARBUTHNOTT

26 AUGUST 2006

'There's a dry wind blowing through the East and the parched grasses wait and spark.' This is not the sort of language we associate with a high-ranking official in the Foreign Office, but things were different in 1916. Not altogether different, however. 'Islam is a fighting creed, and the mullah still stands in the pulpit with the Koran in one hand and a drawn sword in the other. Supposing there is some Ark of the Covenant which will madden the remotest Moslem peasant with dreams of Paradise? What then?' 'Then there will be hell let loose in these parts pretty soon.'

Happily, for this is fiction, that hell will be arrested, the dry wind calmed, thanks to the efforts of our four heroes: a South African mining engineer of Scots extraction, the Eton- and Oxford-educated younger son of a Scottish peer, a dyspeptic American whose eyes have previously 'seen nothing gorier than a Presidential election', and an Afrikaner hunter with a dubious past: 'He had been in Swaziland with Bob Macnab, and you know what that means.' Actually this is the only mention of Bob Macnab in *Greenmantle*, but the throwaway line is typical of John Buchan's cavalier way. It is indeed one of my favourite lines in the canon, even if it doesn't quite match Sandy Arbuthnott's sublime observation in *The Three Hostages*: 'Nothing wastes time like dodging assassins.' How true, how very true. Those who endured the recent chaos at our airports will nod their heads in agreement.

The plot of *Greenmantle* is, even by Buchan's standards, absurd. Richard Hannay is commissioned, despite his ignorance of the East

— 'I never saw a Turk in my life except a chap who did wrestling turns in a show in Kimberley' — to prevent the Germans from stirring up a Holy War or *Jihad*. (Buchan spells it *Jehad*.) Time is short. He meets that evening the American, John S. Blenkiron, and Sandy Arbuthnott (modelled on Aubrey Herbert, grandfather, among other claims to fame, of Auberon Waugh). It is 17 November. 'If we can't find out what we want in two months we may chuck the job. On 17 January we should foregather in Constantinople.' Considering that all have to get there by devious routes, this is a tight itinerary. Hannay himself, posing as an Afrikaner eager to resume fighting the British, must go first to Lisbon, there attract the interest of German agents, then be shipped to Germany as a useful man, win the confidence of the authorities and persuade them to send him to Constantinople. Tough going.

Coincidences abound. No writer of what Buchan called 'shockers' disdains coincidence. It is a way of keeping the story moving and of getting your hero out of difficulties or, alternatively, into them. But Buchan's use of coincidence is splendidly shameless. Hannay, for instance, meets his old friend the Boer hunter Peter Pienaar just by chance in Lisbon; later, after they have been separated by the Germans, he encounters him again sitting on the banks of the Danube hoping to thumb a lift to the Bosphorus. Hannay, Blenkiron and Peter all do their bit, but the key man is Sandy who, fortunately, 'can pass anywhere as a Turk'. He is the sort of chap you hear about 'at little forgotten fishing ports where the Albanian mountains meet the Adriatic, and if you struck a Mecca pilgrimage the odds are you would meet a dozen of Sandy's friends in it.' Sandy can even assume the role of the prophet 'Greenmantle', the novel's Osama bin Laden figure, when the real Greenmantle dies, conveniently, of cancer.

When Buchan wrote *Greenmantle* and for decades afterwards, his nightmare vision of a resurgent Islam and a new *Jihad* seemed out of date, mere romantic melodrama. Arab nationalism, not Islam, was the idea on the march: Arab nationalism and Arab socialism. Nasser and the various Ba'athist leaders like Saddam Hussein had little time for Islam. It was backward, and they were all for modernity. Sandy, naturally, was wiser:

> The West knows nothing of the true Oriental. The Kâf he yearns for is an austere thing. It is the austerity of the East that is its beauty and its terror. The Turk and the Arab came out of big spaces, and they have the desire of them in their bones... They want to prune life of its foolish fringes and get back to the noble bareness of the desert.

Maybe *Greenmantle* should be a set book for our security services. It might help them understand what we are up against. It may indeed help us all to understand why middle-class Muslim boys reared in this country turn against it and all our ways, in thrall to 'the prophet of this great simplicity'.

A WAY WITH WORDS

9 SEPTEMBER 2006

In his essay *Politics and the English Language* George Orwell translated a well-known verse from Ecclesiastes into modern English, producing this:

> Objective consideration of contemporary phenomena compels the conclusion that success or failure in competitive activities exhibits no tendency to be commensurate with innate capacity, but that a considerable element of the unpredictable must invariably be taken into account.

This is pretty dreadful, though I have a suspicion that a twenty-first-century version offered by a government department would be even worse. But it does serve to remind us that how you say something is at least as important as what you say.

Here is another example: 'The war continued to be waged throughout the autumn months, but we were no longer actively engaged in the conflict.' 'In the Fall the war was always there, but we did not go to it anymore.' The meaning of these two sentences is the same, but the effect on the reader is different. The first is clear enough, but merely informative; there is an emotional charge to the second, which is (as you will remember) the opening line of a Hemingway short story.

How you say something may, however, matter less in prose than verse. Novels can be translated satisfactorily. No doubt Dostoevsky in Russian has something to offer which you don't find in an English version, but this gives you enough to be compelling. In any case, as Somerset Maugham observed, some great novelists (he instanced Balzac, Dickens and Dostoevsky) often write their own language very clumsily. (Did he say clumsily or badly? I can't remember.)

Poetry is different. 'Poetry,' Housman wrote, 'is not the thing said but a way of saying it.' For example: 'Let us go then, you and I,/ When the evening is spread out against the sky/ Like a patient etherised upon a table.' Does this make sense? Early readers of Eliot thought not. How on earth, they angrily said, can the evening sky be thought to resemble a hospital patient lying on an operating table? Fair enough: the comparison is indeed absurd. Yet the lines work, they stick in the mind, they are poetry.

But how would they sound in translation? Can poetry indeed be translated? *'Quis multa gracilis te puer in rosa/ Perfusus liquidis urget odoribus/ Grato, Pyrrha, sub antro?' The Penguin Book of Latin Verse* offers this translation: 'What slender lad, bathed in liquid perfumes, courts thee, Pyrrha, in a pleasant cave on a couch of roses?' This is accurate enough. We have the meaning, but the poetry has evaporated. You get the sense of the passage, but no idea of why, for 2,000 years, Horace has delighted those capable of reading him in his own tongue.

If a poem is never just the thing said but the way of saying it, then the translator must be a poet himself and what he makes will be a new poem deriving from the original. Here is another example from Horace, the opening of the Ode, *Diffugere nives.* The Penguin version of the first verse goes as follows: 'The snows have fled. The grass is returning to the fields and the leaves to the trees. Earth is running through her changes, and the rivers flow past their banks with declining strength.' Clear enough, but no more than that. Housman made this of it: 'The snows have fled away, leaves on the shaws, /And grasses in the mead renew their birth,/ The river to the river-bed withdraws,/ And altered is the fashion of the earth.'

Translation is good practise for the apprentice poet; it saves him from the trouble of thinking what to say, allows him to concentrate on 'the way of saying it'. Sometimes the translator poet is fortunate, and makes a true poem in his own language. The magical wand has rested on him. Everyone knows William Johnson Cory's version of Callimachus's lament for his dead friend: 'They told me, Heraclitus, they told me you were dead . . .'

Here is another version, less well-known, but to my mind as good. It is by Charles Murray who wrote in the Doric of his native Aberdeenshire: 'They taul' me, Heraclitus, that ye had worn awa';/ I grat to mind hoo aft we ca'd the crack atween the twa/ Until the heark'nin' sun gaed doon news-weary i' the Wast:/ An' noo for lang ye're in the mools, whaur a' maun lie at last./ Still, still they pipe your mavises, though sair the Makker's miss't,/ For Death that coffins a' the lave your sangs can never kist.' Cory's nightingales become mavises — that is, the mistle-thrush. The last word 'kist' is a box or chest, hence a coffin, usually a noun, here serving as a verb. Perhaps you need to have heard and spoken the Doric as a child fully to appreciate this version. But that merely proves that 'poetry is not the thing said but a way of saying it'.

THE ORIGINAL DYLAN

23 SEPTEMBER 2006

The suggestion was made the other day that Dylan Thomas may have been dyslexic. Apparently, the experts deduced this from the style of his poetry. It seems an odd assertion. Dyslexic children find difficulty, and therefore no pleasure, in reading. Dylan, according to his parents, taught himself to read when he was three, and thereafter read, in his own words, 'indiscriminatingly and all the time, with my eyes hanging out on stalks'. Doesn't sound like a dyslexic child to me, though doubtless the experts know better. Also in the news recently was the announcement of a Dylan Thomas Prize, worth £50,000 to the winner. Considering that having failed to file a tax return for years before the Inland Revenue caught up with him and sank its claws in so deeply that from 1948 to his death in November 1953 'he was never, for a single day', according to his biographer Constantine Fitzgibbon, 'free of financial terror', the value of this prize seems like a bad joke.

It's difficult now, when the name Dylan has more people thinking first of the American songster than the Welsh poet, to convey to the young just how famous Dylan Thomas was half a century ago, and why. His poetry wasn't easily accessible like Betjeman's; it was rhetorical, high-flown, romantic, and sometimes it didn't, as poets like Larkin and Kingsley Amis (both a few years younger), irritably complained, make sense. Certainly, sense is not always easy to extract from it, though it always made a splendid sound, which is more than can be said for Larkin's and Amis's own verse. The high sales of his *Collected Poems* (10,000 in the first year, 20,000 in the second, after his death) probably owed as much to the legend of the wild, dissolute, doomed poet as to the work, though the same observation can't be applied to the hugely successful play *Under Milk Wood*.

The stories of his American tours, of his drunkenness and wild behaviour, fed the legend, and then his death, following his boast, 'I've had 18 straight whiskies — I think that's the record', confirmed it. It was a sort of suicide, people said; he destroyed himself because he was written out. In short, for the early Fifties, Dylan played the part that rock stars were to do later; he was our generation's Jim Morrison or Pete Doherty.

The American poet James Dickey put the case against him in a *Paris Review* interview: 'Thomas didn't write one poem in the last six years of his life . . . Why should he write another book of poems and maybe give the critics another shot at him that would lower his reading fee?' A judgment both malicious and inaccurate. Poems were still written. As his widow Caitlin says, 'They were taking him longer to finish than they had ever done before, but they were far better poems for it.' In any case, the publication of the *Collected Poems* gave any critic the chance to shoot at him; in fact the reception of the book would only have raised that reading fee.

Drink and financial anxiety — the two horribly connected — were at the root of his troubles, and it was booze that killed him, with a bit of help from the incompetence of the doctors in New York. What makes the thought of his early death still bitter is that the financial troubles were nearly behind him. The *Collected Poems* and *Under Milk Wood* would have given him freedom from the gnawing anxiety. Caitlin came to believe that with this burden lifted 'he would have sorted himself out and brought his drinking under control because all the things that made him drink were coming under control as well'. That may be so. My view has always been that there was nothing wrong with him that knocking off the booze wouldn't have enabled him to put right.

I used to know Caitlin when I was living in Rome in the early Seventies. She was in AA by then and social life was a torment to her, but she was very kind and generous to me at a difficult time in my own life. No doubt she had been different in her drinking days — hot-tempered, quarrelsome and demanding, by many accounts — but I found her gentle and understanding. I never asked her about Dylan. Of course now I wish I had, but it seemed that the memories were still too painful, and I think that she had suffered from living in the reflection of his glamour.

As for the poetry, I still read it with enjoyment, admiration and puzzlement, and relish the prefatory note to the *Collected Poems*:

> I read somewhere of a shepherd who, when asked why he made, from within fairy rings, ritual advances to the moon to protect his flocks, replied 'I'd be a damn' fool if I didn't!' These poems, with all their crudities, doubts and confusions, are written for the love of Man and in praise of God, and I'd be a damn' fool if they weren't.

THE LAST TIME HE SAW PARIS

7 OCTOBER 2006

One good reason to read Simenon is to recover Paris. It is now 75 years since Maigret made his first appearance, and, if his Paris is not yet utterly lost, you have to walk distances and search diligently to find it. The Brasserie Dauphine, for instance, rue de Harlay, which in real life was the Restaurant aux Trois Marches, is now the restaurant-salon of the Paris Bar (La Maison du Barreau). Maigret's favourite *blanquette de veau* may still be simmering there, but consumption will be reserved to lawyers.

Though fond of the district Maubert-Mouffetard, in his day a poor quarter, Maigret is essentially a man of the Right Bank: of the faubourg Saint-Antoine and the Marais, a *quartier de petits gens* and Jewish immigrants, of artisan workshops and small, disreputable hotels. Much has changed. The Marais has been gentrified, and is now the gay quarter. Something of the atmosphere Maigret knew may still be caught, but you are more likely now to find it in Belleville and off the Boulevard Rochechouart and Boulevard Barbès, districts where your typical Parisian is no longer white.

Maigret is also at home the length of the Canal Saint-Martin, which has changed less, as indeed has the faubourg Saint-Antoine, and much of the XIe with its little streets and impasses, and of course the Boulevard Richard Lenoir where, at No. 132 on the third floor, Madame Maigret is waiting to open the door for him as soon as she hears his step on the stair.

Maigret is rarely at ease in Montparnasse, still less so in the wealthy bourgeois quarters of the VIIIe and XVIe. Summoned there, he can never quite forget his peasant background, that his father was a *régisseur du château* (that is a steward or bailiff on an estate) in the Bourbonnais. Yet he is fond of the Île Saint-Louis, because it seems to house a community and to retain an air of provincial peace. Besides, he loves the river and the contrast between the lives of the river people and the clochards who sleep under the bridges, and the rich who inhabit the lovely seventeenth-century houses, quai d'Anjou, quai d'Orleans.

Simenon indeed keeps returning to the Île. One of the best of his *roman durs*, the novels without Maigret, is partly set there. This is *En Cas de Malheur*, the story of the infatuation of the star lawyer Gobillot, living in the Hôtel de Lauzun, quai d'Anjou, with a teenage criminal, Yvette. It was filmed with Jean Gabin and Brigitte Bardot — a movie I should love to see, for both were, one imagines, exactly right for the roles. Incidentally, you can still eat in the restaurant they frequent, Chez Manière, rue Caulaincourt in Montmartre, though it now goes by another name which I forget. Back on the Île Saint-Louis, Maigret would, I fancy, still approve of the Alsatian Brasserie by the Pont Saint-Louis, where the *choucroute garni* is as good as at Lipp.

One needs no excuse to be a *flâneur* in Paris, though Simenon provides us with one, and indeed Maigret himself is a *flâneur*. It is by his immersion in the daily life around him that characteristically he arrives at the solution of crimes.

At a time when crime novels are often stretched to 400 pages or even more, it is a relief, as well as a pleasure, to return to the Maigret novels, so brief, so clear in their narrative, so uncluttered. It's not that Maigret disdains what we now call forensic science. Indeed in the very first Maigret, *Pietr le Letton*, we are assured that he 'made use of the extraordinary tools that the Berillons, Reisses and Locards have put in the hands of the police, and which constitute a veritable science. But' — the qualification is important

— 'but he waited and watched for the moment of the crack, when behind the player appeared the man.' It is Simenon's empathy, his understanding of how people behave when stretched to breaking-point, that lift the Maigret novels high above the common run of crime fiction, even indeed the best of it.

If they are strangely comforting books — the late historian Richard Cobb called them reassuring — it is partly because of the sense of felt life, partly because of Maigret's sympathy and reluctance to condemn. But it is also because of the affection with which the setting is realised. Of the 76 Maigret novels, 63 are set in Paris, wholly or in part, and reading them enriches one's experience of the city. But Maigret's is not the tourists' Paris or the historical Paris or the Paris of 'cultural attractions'. It is the people and their daily life that obsess him. He loves habit, and, happily, reading the Maigret novels becomes a habit, one of which I at least have never tired.

A MASTER CARPENTER

21 OCTOBER 2006

Who did Evelyn Waugh call 'the only living studio-master under whom one can study with profit'? Answer: Somerset Maugham. Surprising answer? Perhaps. Others judged him more harshly; Edmund Wilson dismissed him as 'a half-trashy novelist who writes badly, but is patronised by half-serious readers who do not care much about writing.' Actually Maugham took a lot of trouble over his writing, as his notebooks show. They, incidentally, like Wilson's own notebooks, are full of descriptive passages in embarrassingly purple prose. Hard to see the point of them; when did either author think he might take one of these passages and shove it into a novel? Maugham also resorts to cliché, on almost every page. This is not necessarily a bad thing, in moderation anyway. Clichés don't distract the reader from the narrative, as more original and highly charged language may.

Waugh explained his admiration. Reviewing *Christmas Holiday* (1939), he wrote that 'one reads it with a feeling of increasing respect for his mastery of the trade. One has the same delight as in watching a first-class cabinet-maker cutting dovetails.' Waugh was, first and last, a craftsman, and if poverty hadn't driven him into the family business, which was writing, would have been a cabinet-maker.

It's years since I read *Christmas Holiday*, and I can't lay my hands on a copy; never mind. There's another novel, *Cakes and Ale*, so expertly and pleasingly constructed that it makes Waugh's point. The opening sentences catch you straightaway

34

A MASTER CARPENTER

I have noticed that when someone asks for you on the telephone, and, finding you out, leaves a message begging you to call him up the moment you come in, and it's important, the matter is more often important to him than to you. When it comes to making you a present or doing you a favour most people are able to hold their impatience within reasonable bounds.

The tone is established: this is the worldly-wise Mr Maugham, thinly disguised as Willie Ashenden, opening a little comedy for you.

The call is from a successful man of letters, Alroy Kear, and Maugham has a lovely time explaining how he can think of none of his contemporaries who 'had achieved so considerable a reputation on so little talent'. There can scarcely be a novelist who hasn't wanted to depict such a figure. It was taken to be a cruel portrait of Hugh Walpole. Maugham denied it then, later admitting he had had Walpole in mind. Now this matters not a jot. Walpole is dead, and Alroy Kear gloriously alive.

He has undertaken to write the life of a distinguished novelist, Edward Driffield, whom Ashenden knew as a boy when the young Ted Driffield lived in the Kentish town where Ashenden's uncle was the vicar. Will he jot down his memories? Opportunity for mischief: Roy and the second Mrs Driffield are very respectable — 'I see this rather like a portrait by Van Dyke,' Roy says, 'with a deal of atmosphere, you know, and a certain gravity, and with a sort of aristocratic distinction.' But the young Driffield and his first wife, Rosie, were anything but respectable.

The contrast between the book Roy will write and the reality is nicely made in this exchange: 'And you saw a good deal of him later in London, I believe.' 'Yes.' 'That is when he had an apartment somewhere in Lower Belgravia.' 'Well, lodgings in Pimlico.'

The novel alternates between the present, when Ashenden is middle-aged, and his memories of adolescence in Blackstable and early years in London, the two periods of his life when he knew Ted and Rosie. Manipulating a double time-scale while maintaining the reader's interest in both the then and the now is one of the hardest tasks a novelist can set himself. Maugham brings it off with enviable dexterity, teasing his story out until he reveals to the reader, but not to Roy and the widow, the 'bombshell' Ashenden could have thrown if he chose.

It's full of nice observation about changing manners and morals, wit and humour, well-drawn and interesting characters, and told in just the right tone of voice, but it's Maugham's mastery of the structure and his ability to modulate the pace that make it one of our great comic novels — a very fine piece of carpentry indeed. There are three and a half dead pages in the middle (168–171 in my Everyman's Library edition). Otherwise it is perfect. But I'm amazed Maugham didn't cut that passage.

WHAT PRICE
GEORGE MEREDITH?

4 NOVEMBER 2006

Another biography of Thomas Hardy, and, it seems a good one, by Claire Tomalin. But what is it about Hardy that so attracts biographers? There have been a good few of them, even in the last quarter century. Indeed Hardy ('little Tommy Hardy', as Henry James unkindly and not very sensibly called him) has survived rather well. His novels are regularly set for A-level and several have been filmed. His poetry too has lasted. What G. M. Young called its 'ancient music . . . this gnarled and wintry phrasing' endures, influencing, for instance, Philip Larkin.

And what of his contemporary rival poet-novelist, with whom his name was coupled, and to whom he was compared? What of Meredith? Down in the cellar with no takers. Meredith, Paul Johnson informed us recently, was 'no good'. Others seem to agree. Moreover, though his life was at least as interesting as Hardy's, he attracts no biographers. I remember reviewing one near the end of the Seventies. Has there been another since? Strange: this, after all, was a novelist whom Stevenson regarded as a master, and one whom James declared 'very superior to any other here, in his scorn for the beefy British public and all its vulgarities and brutalities'.

As for his biography, not many English novelists have been exhibited at the Royal Academy impersonating a dying poet, but Meredith was the model for Henry Wallis's famous painting *The Death of Chatterton*. Sadly for Meredith, his first wife, who was the daughter of Thomas Love Peacock, then ran off with the painter. This provoked his poetic sequence, *Modern Love*, which is witty, intelligent and painful. 'How many a thing which we cast to the ground/ When others pick it up becomes a gem.'

Like Hardy, Meredith seems to have thought of himself as a poet first and novelist second, though, unlike Hardy, he pursued both careers concurrently. Some of the verse is pretty dreadful, but that may be said of any prolific poet. 'Was there ever such stuff as great part of Shakespeare?' George III asked Fanny Burney, before adding prudently, 'Only one must not say so.' Meredith's worst is no worse than the worst of Tennyson and Browning, and his best is exhilarating. 'She whom I love is hard to catch and conquer,/ Hard, but O the glory of the winning were she won.'

The novels are sometimes hard work, principally on account of Meredith's style, which is elliptical and epigrammatic. I confess to having been bogged down in *The Egoist* more than once. But it is worth persevering. As Gore Vidal, an admirer, wrote, 'Meredith's energy, wit, comic invention are not only satisfying but like no one else's.' And the style is certainly no more difficult than Proust's and less so than Joyce's.

If *The Egoist* can be hard going, this isn't true of *Beauchamp's Career*, arguably the finest of Victorian political novels, which is saying something, for competition from Disraeli and Trollope is stiff, or of Rhoda Fleming, or my own favourite, *The Adventures of Harry Richmond*. This has its absurdities — the school scenes now seem as far-fetched as, well, school scenes in any Victorian novel — but there is a wonderful gusto to the whole book and it rattles along at a marvellous pace. I suppose it may fairly be called a romance, rather than a novel, and the central figure, Harry's father, Richmond Roy, with his wild boast of royal blood and claim to be the rightful king of England, strains credulity — except when you are caught up in the story. This con-man and adventurer is a creation worthy of Dumas. The novel benefits from being written, unlike most of Meredith's, in the first person, and if permitted to keep only half a dozen novels from the Victorian age, *Harry Richmond* would be one of my selections, which wouldn't, however, include any of Hardy's.

Considering the popularity of Hardy and the eclipse of Meredith, I conclude that this is because Hardy's view of life is deeply gloomy, despondent and therefore serious, whereas Meredith's is cheerful and vigorous. To Hardy it's a tragedy, to Meredith it's a comedy. For Hardy life is something to be endured; for Meredith a challenge. It's true that he published one book entitled *Ballads and Poems of Tragic Life*, but they are not very convincing. You feel his heart isn't in it. Exuberance keeps breaking in. This tells against him. We all know, don't we, that a serious writer must see life as ugly, disappointing, even pointless. What puzzles me is that Paul Johnson doesn't respond to Meredith.

PAPA RISES AGAIN

18 NOVEMBER 2006

We were in a Béarnais restaurant in Montmartre and a young Canadian novelist and short story writer, Bill Prendiville, was speaking admiringly about Hemingway. This was pleasing, because you don't often hear him being praised now. It was also appropriate, because most of the good early Hemingway was written in Paris, and the best of his later books is his memoir of Paris in the Twenties. Admittedly his Paris was the Left Bank — rue Cardinal Lemoine, Boulevard Saint-Germain, rue Mouffetard, Montparnasse — rather than up in the 18th, and some of the books Bill spoke warmly of are not among those I like. Still, it was good to hear him spoken of in this way.

As with Dylan Thomas, the legend gets in the way of the literature, and Hemingway the celebrity, boastful, brutal, dishonest, and talking his Hollywood Indian language, is a fairly awful, even repulsive figure. Sadly, the more one learns the clearer it is that the private Hemingway was often every bit as nasty.

I used to think differently. Reading A. E. Hotchner's *Papa* almost 40 years ago, I would have given much to have been included in his entourage. 'Let us resume the having of the fun' — oh yes, please. Hotchner's last chapters are of course grim and painful, all the fun evaporated, never to be resumed. The account of the last years when he was crazy, paranoid, miserable, but still trying doggedly to write, is pathetic, even tragic, Hemingway resembling — to adopt a suitable image — a bloodied and puzzled bull, head brought low by the picadors, waiting for the matador's final thrust to end the agony.

PAPA RISES AGAIN

Despite the Nobel Prize, his reputation, as distinct from celebrity, was on the slide long before he shot himself in 1961. Wilfrid Sheed wrote that 'his serious admirers had retreated by then to defending the early short stories and parts of *The Sun Also Rises*, and snippets of *A Farewell to Arms*, and retreat usually leads to rout in these matters; the short stories could not hold out by themselves for ever.' (Actually they can, still reading as if new-minted.) But *Across the River and Into the Trees* had been panned by the critics, though Raymond Chandler had a good word for it.

Apart from the Big Fish novella, that was the last novel he published. Several have come out posthumously, editors reassembling and shaping a mass of often incoherent material. In most cases one sees why and how Hemingway got stuck, and the books go some way to supporting the view that he was a burnt-out case.

There was one exception, a novella, *The Garden of Eden*. 'They were living at le Grau du Roi then and the hotel was on a canal that ran from the walled city of Aigues Mortes down to the sea.' They were David and Catherine, and they are newly married and happy, and he is a young writer tasting his first success. So they are at ease in the Eden of young love. But it is not as simple as that. They play games with their sexual identity, so that sometimes he is Catherine and she is Peter, and at other times she is a boy who likes to be called 'Devil'. They pick up another girl who first sleeps with Catherine before Catherine insists that David makes her his other wife. It is a story of the corruption of innocence, but it ends with David writing more truly than ever before.

It is good, and one wonders why he never published it. My guess is that he was alarmed to discover how he had revealed too much of himself, offered ammunition to his enemies. Nobody ever doubted Hemingway's physical courage, but moral courage is another matter, and it was perhaps timidity that had him lock the manuscript away.

41

Yet it reminds one where his true talent, indeed genius, lay, and, in doing so, shows where he went wrong. He was a master at revealing states of mind and feeling through dialogue, and at finding what Eliot called 'the objective correlative'. From the start he distrusted the big words, but his public persona and the demands of critics pushed him towards writing the Big Novel. He wasn't equipped to do this; he was a miniaturist, which is why the short stories, where there is no room for development, remain so fresh and good. In *The Garden of Eden* there is no showing off, no 'getting into the ring with Mr Tolstoy'. It's the genuine article, the work of a scrupulous and dedicated artist, and it's good if some writers are now speaking up for him. As for his character, who says artists must be nice people? Think of Wagner.

ROTH MARCHES ON

2 DECEMBER 2006

Writing here (18 November), Anita Brookner described Joseph Roth's reports from France 1925–39, *The White Cities*, as 'her best read of the year'. I've had a copy for several months now, and I keep dipping into it and always finding something new, surprising and delightful. The rediscovery of Roth has been one of the happiest things in recent years; it owes much to the devotion and excellence of his translator, Michael Hofmann, and of course to the support given by his publisher, Granta.

Roth is probably best known for *The Radetzky March*, one of the masterpieces of twentieth-century fiction. None of his other books may match that; why should they? — it's enough to have written one such novel; but nothing he wrote is less than fresh, illuminating and original, and everything, fiction and journalism alike, is completely individual, the voice unmistakable.

The White Cities offers not only delightful pictures of France between the wars; it is also the record of the impact of the country and society on one born a subject of the Habsburg empire (to the memory of which he remained loyal), then, after 1933, a refugee from Nazi Germany. As a journalist Roth has an enviably light touch, comes at things from unexpected angles. Some pieces are harrowing, the Thirties being what they were. One article, *Children of Exile*, recounts a conversation with an eight-year-old boy, son of an Austrian Jewish shoemaker, met in the waiting-room of a police prefecture in Paris. The boy has learned more of the world than he should have at his age, understands it better perhaps than his father. The article was written in October 1938, a month after Munich, and this is how Roth ends it:

> I've just seen a photograph, printed in several newspapers, of a little English girl who apparently had been waiting since ten in the morning for Neville Chamberlain and his wife, and finally got to meet them in the afternoon, and, on behalf of all British children, to express her thanks to the British prime minister for going to Germany on his peace missions. A sweet little English girl ... God grant that she never comes into the sort of knowledge that the eight-year-old son of my Austrian shoemaker has come into.

The juxtapositioning, sharp yet strangely delicate, of these two stories, is characteristic.

I don't suppose Roth will ever be a popular writer; he wasn't in his own lifetime. In September 1937 he noted the arrival of his eighteenth book: 'of the previous 17, 15 have been forgotten'. Three days later he gets the royalty statement for his 17th one: 3,450 copies sold. 'I am a long way from having "earned back" my advance.' His publisher writes sadly, 'It's terrible to see these accounts'. Roth reflects:

> And I'm not their only author. My colleagues' advances are not covered either. Book publishing is a weird and wonderful business. Publishers deal in red figures. It must be very hard, especially when you bear in mind that I can't live off my advances either.

One knows just what he means and how he feels.

I have developed a special reverence for Roth. Few writers have better displayed that quality Hemingway admired: grace under pressure. And the pressure to which Roth was subjected was greater and more intense than most of us, in our prosperous and generally tolerant Europe, can imagine. So also was the temptation to despair, which nevertheless he resisted. Humour keeps breaking through, wry, ironical humour, astringent certainly, but also often tender.

So, whenever I am in Paris I go to the Café de Tournon, just below the Luxembourg Gardens about which he wrote so well and lovingly, and drink a cup of coffee to his memory at the table where he drank stronger liquors. I don't know if it is the café which he described in *The Bistro after Midnight*, but I like to think it is the place where he listened to the old taxi-driver who was once a coachman and who told him what was wrong with the world: 'It's conscience — conscience has been eradicated. It's been replaced by authorisation' — an observation worth pondering today also.

A WORLD OF SNOBS
AND SWINDLERS

16 DECEMBER 2006

Orwell thought that Mark Twain's picture of life on the Mississippi showed 'how human beings behave when they are not frightened of the sack' and so are free to develop their personalities. Something similar might be said of the rural England portrayed by R. S. Surtees, even if in his novels household servants, grooms and huntsmen may be in danger of being 'turned off without a character'. Nevertheless Orwell's observation that in Twain's Mississippi stories 'the State hardly existed' while 'the churches were weak and spoke with many voices' might be applied to Surtees's England too.

Reading *Mr Sponge's Sporting Tour* again, one is struck by the complete absence of officialdom. There is poverty there. The peasants — and they are really peasants whom Surtees calls 'chawbacons' — are a miserable lot. And yet this is an England where people are free as we are not today. They lead unsupervised lives. The State neither afflicts nor cossets them. They are not required to fill in government forms, or prove their identity to anyone. Nor, though Sponge was published well into Victoria's reign, in 1853, does religion play any part in his characters' lives. Parsons are met at the dinner table or in the hunting field, but not in the pulpit.

Admittedly the picture Surtees gives of mid-nineteenth-century England, while convincing, is also limited and partial. Difficult to remember while deep in the novel that 100 miles or so from the rough squires, crooked horse-dealers and gulls whom he describes with such relish, Puseyites were arguing about the precise interpretation to be put on the 39 Articles of Religion, Carlyle was fulminating in Chelsea about the cash nexus, and Darwin was brooding on the mysteries of evolution. But of course no novelist ever gives a full picture of society; it's enough that he presents his chosen segment persuasively, and few have done this better than Surtees.

Sponge is a novel you can dip into, read a couple of chapters with pleasure, and lay aside. I have been treating it like this for more years, especially more winters, than I care to remember. There is a narrative, the story jogs along, but there is no plot. It's pure picaresque. Inasmuch as there is a plan, it is simple. Our hero, Mr Sponge ('Soapey' to his friends) is not quite a gentleman; he is a wide boy and a fortune-hunter. With a couple of hired hacks — ill-tempered, hard-to-manage brutes such as only a horseman as fine as Sponge can control — he imposes himself on a series of country squires in order to indulge his passion for hunting and, he hopes, snare a well-endowed bride. His horses are for sale — at a price — and he will take them back — for a consideration — when the buyer he has fooled finds them too much for him.

What makes the book so satisfying and enjoyable is first, as I say, the completeness with which Surtees brings this uncouth rural society before us, and, second, his mastery of detail. He is wonderfully good not only on horses, but on clothes, houses, meals, weather. His prose rambles, sometimes ungrammatically, but his ear for dialogue is sharp, and his characters live in their speech. He is brilliant at portraying snobs, social climbers, parasites, humbugs. Sponge himself is a swindler with few redeeming features, quite lacking in charm, but somehow we are on his side, even when he combines with another man to cheat and bully a wretched youth called Pacey. Surtees has no sympathy for the victim: Pacey is a vain fool, and deserves all he gets.

The tone is consistently sardonic. Surtees has no illusions, no time for cant. His world is tough and hard, and though he writes with contempt for the fools and scoundrels who inhabit it, he does so with irresistible relish. Sponge is his best book, by some way, one you can cut into at any point and never exhaust — rather like *Pickwick* and *Vanity Fair* in this respect.

Joyce Cary, in an excellent introduction to the old World's Classics edition, wrote that '*Sponge* is not a book for the sentimentalist', and this is generally true. Yet the ending may be called sentimental, for Sponge marries and looks set to live happily ever after. Admittedly his bride is not the well-dowried girl he had looked for, but a showgirl called Lucy Glitters, perhaps the only heroine in Victorian fiction to be described as 'tolerably virtuous'. She is, however, also beautiful, and more evidently desirable than most nineteenth-century heroines. She and Sponge are well-matched and set up 'a splendid establishment in Jermyn Street, St James's, now known as the Sponge Cigar and Betting Rooms'. Would it was still there, inviting us to 'indulge in one of Lucy's unrivalled cigars'!

NO LADIES' MAN

6 JANUARY 2007

'Walter Scott is unjust towards love; there is no force or colour in his account of it, no energy. One can see that he has studied it in books and not in his own heart.' That was Stendhal's opinion, and many even of Scott's most devoted readers would not dissent from it. Dialogues between his young lovers are, to put it mildly, rarely satisfactory. The idea of his young heroines may be pleasing. One can understand why Victorian schoolboys are said to have fallen in love with Diana Vernon in *Rob Roy*; she is beautiful, lively and resourceful, a fine horsewoman and gallant Jacobite.

John Buchan also succumbed to her spell: 'Not only is the reader vividly conscious of her charm of person and manner and her fineness of spirit, but he is aware of a notable intelligence.' Alas, the spell doesn't work for me. Indeed, this is to see her as Frank Osbaldistone, the young narrator, sees her, not as she reveals herself. The charm dissolves when she speaks; her language is dull and formal, even pompous. There is no vitality in it. She is, as A. O. J. Cockshut wrote in one of the best books about Scott, 'a day dream'; or, if you like, a Bond girl. Scott himself knew that he was no great hand at depicting young ladies, partly, I think, because he did not hear their voices in his head, partly, perhaps because he had too much respect for them — and for the proprieties — but principally because, as Stendhal suggested, the idea of love did not fire his imagination.

Nevertheless his heroines made an impression on his early readers. A few months ago I discovered a book in a second-hand shop (appropriately in Melrose) which substantiates this claim.

49

Galerie des Femmes de Walter Scott, Quarante-Deux Portraits, accompagnés chacun d'un portrait littéraire was published in Paris in 1839, seven years after his death. No editor is named, but the publisher is given as Ambroise Dupont, 7 Rue Vivienne. Most of the authors of the essays were, I suspect, hacks but there are two pieces by Dumas and five by Mme Desbordes Valmore, a poet 'whose true value', *The Oxford Companion to Literature in French* tells me, 'has been acknowledged only in relatively recent times', though she was praised also by Baudelaire and Verlaine.

The tone of the articles is generally enthusiastic, the admired heroines being often addressed personally. The first piece (on Diana Vernon again) is characteristic:

> Ah! You have guessed it, Diana, you weren't made for that cold England, where life runs, like the wagons of Liverpool, on two rails — custom and convention — where all the aspirations of the will, all the thirsts of the soul are brought up short against one word: improper! ... No, you couldn't live in that atmosphere of constraint and dissimulation. You were right to become French and to change your name.

Actually Frank Osbaldistone follows her to France, retrieves her from the convent to which she had withdrawn, and marries her. No matter; the author of the panegyric knows that, whatever name Diana may now go by, 'France admires you and loves you'.

Dumas, not surprisingly, is more astute in his reading of Flora MacIvor, the true heroine of *Waverley*. She is, he says, of an age when all nature — the murmuring stream, the sighing wind, the chanting birds — seem to say: 'Love'. 'And yet, whoever you are, don't go to speak to her of love. For she is wild as a mountaineer and proud as a queen ... for all her love is for her brother.' Dumas himself, one might add, is no great shakes at portraying young ladies. Think how colourless Louise de la Vallière is in that otherwise splendid novel *Le Vicomte de Bragelonne*.

Rebecca, the Jewish heroine of Ivanhoe, has so overwhelmed the author assigned to her that he addresses her tenderly in the second person singular. He sees her as a finely tragic figure, caught up in a sad, deep and silent love. 'The virgin who has never loved can weep over the unknown love of which she dreams, but you, poor Rebecca, know who your love is, and you know that you will never get him.' The same author, Frédéric Soulié, wrote also about Rebecca's rival, the lovely Saxon Rowena, and so intense is his feeling that he seems almost to be rewriting the novel itself. As it happens he was a successful writer of *romans-feuilletons*, novels published as serials in newspapers and magazines, and his own work owed much to Scott. But then almost everyone's did. As Simenon remarked, after expressing surprise that such a monument as Scott's in Princes Street should have been put up 'to one of us, a novelist . . . After all, why not? He invented us all'.

THE REWARDS OF CRIME

20 JANUARY 2007

Raymond Chandler once praised Dashiell Hammett for having given murder back to the sort of people who committed it. One knows what he meant; away with murders at the vicarage or on the Orient Express (where, however, a good few have doubtless taken place). Yet it wasn't really a very intelligent observation because all sorts of people, even little old ladies and clergymen, do in fact commit murder. In any case, what used to be called 'the hard-boiled crime novel', even Chandler's own, marvellous as the best three or four of them are, is often as far from realism as the classic English detective novel. Marlowe himself is a romanticised figure, which is why he was best played by Bogart, and the Hollywood scenes in that sometimes brilliant but flawed novel, *The Little Sister*, are as embarrassing to read now as the exchanges between Lord Peter Wimsey and, well, anyone with whom Wimsey is in conversation.

Nevertheless it's surely unsatisfactory that the crime novel is so often dismissed as 'genre fiction'. Of course most crime novels are poor — but then so are most novels categorised as 'literary'. They may bear reading once, but rarely twice. Again, crime novels, especially those of the police procedural type, are easily weighed down, and often sunk, by pseudo-realistic detail which the reader may well choose to skip. None of this alters the fact that the crime novelist deals with essential and metaphysical realities. That very fine writer, Nicholas Freeling, in a collection of essays entitled *Criminal Convictions*, went so far as to claim that 'in prose fiction, crime is the pre-eminent, and often predominant, theme'.

To prove his point the writers whose work he examines are: Stendhal, Dickens, Conrad, Conan Doyle, Kipling, Chandler, Sayers, Simenon. Only four of the eight are likely to find their books in the crime section of your local bookshop. Yet Freeling makes his argument, cogently to my mind, and might have included books by Scott (*The Heart of Midlothian*), Balzac (almost any volume of *La Comédie Humaine*), Trollope (*The Eustace Diamonds*), Dostoevsky (*Crime and Punishment* and *The Devils*), Ford (*The Good Soldier*) and Greene (*The Quiet American*). 'Crime,' Freeling wrote, 'is the pathology of the human condition, the moment after, it may be, a long drawn-out disturbance or perversion, at which the delicate balance of metabolism tilts into morbidity': an exact definition.

The difficulty for all novelists is to go on. It's not only that you use up material, or that you seem to have said everything before; not only that you may become, as Greene put it, 'the prisoner of your method'. It's that it becomes ever harder to devise new situations and new characters, even to take this task seriously. When this happens, some stop writing; but they are few. Others turn to preaching, concerning themselves with 'social issues'; others abandon the attempt to portray the world as it is, and retreat into extravagance or whimsy. You can see this happening, sadly, with crime novelists whose plots become ever more far-fetched or elaborate, whose criminals seem to amuse themselves with setting fantastic puzzles for the police. The writer who once stayed close to experience and so presented murder as an offence against everything that we value now begins to treat it as a game. This may be entertaining but it is also frivolous. A good example of what I mean is offered by the fashionable French novelist Fred Vargas. Her latest novel, *Wash This Blood from My Hands*, is certainly enjoyable, but, alas, it is no more than high-class hokum because the metaphysical horror of murder — so perfectly realised in *Macbeth* or *Crime and Punishment* — has evaporated. The blood is washed all too easily from the hands.

Today the crime novelist has one advantage denied to writers of 'straight' or 'literary' novels. Unlike them he can range over all levels of society, for crime can easily breach the barriers that exist in our stratified society. Because of these barriers the modern literary novel, unlike its nineteenth-century predecessors, is often confined to the horizontal, dealing only with one class. But crime runs through society from top to bottom, and so the crime novelist can present a fuller picture of the way we live now. His weakness is that, wedded as he often is to a formula and dealing with the same chief characters, there is a tendency for his work to become mechanical, a danger too that he will sentimentalise his central figures. A good example of this is offered by Reginald Hill's Andy Dalziel. Originally a convincing character, tough, clever and rather nasty, he has become in the later books a comic pussy. Nevertheless Hill at his best is one of those who has shown why the crime novel deserves to be taken seriously and not dismissed as genre or entertainment.

WHEN THE JUDGES
GOT IT RIGHT

3 FEBRUARY 2007

In 1907 the Nobel Prize for Literature was for the first time awarded to an English-language writer: Kipling. It wasn't even then a choice that went down well with those whose opinions counted. 'The denizens of literary London,' David Gilmour remarked in *The Last Recessional*, 'were aghast that the prize should have gone to Kipling while Swinburne, Meredith and Hardy were still alive. It was a case, said one of them, of neglecting the goldsmiths and exalting the literary blacksmith.' This was a curious judgment, for, whatever else may be said about Kipling, he was, in the short stories especially, the most careful and cunning craftsman. But by 1907 the youthful virtuosity which had so impressed Robert Louis Stevenson and Henry James had stalled. Literary London was now more conscious of his stridency and 'vulgarity', cruelly and brilliantly parodied by Max Beerbohm. 'It is no use pretending,' Orwell would write in *Horizon* in 1942, 'Kipling's view of life, as a whole, can be accepted or even forgiven by any civilised person … Kipling is a jingo imperialist, he is morally insensitive and aesthetically disgusting.'

No wonder, Orwell continued, 'During five literary generations every enlightened person has despised him.' Nevertheless, Orwell had to admit, 'At the end of that time nine tenths of these enlightened persons are forgotten and Kipling is in some sense still there.' His own essay went on to try to explain why this was the case, and may be seen as an early contribution to the revival of Kipling's reputation. The contribution was limited partly because the essay was a review of Eliot's selection of Kipling's verse, and so paid scant attention to the short stories and none at all to *Kim*. Not many years later Somerset Maugham, with characteristic good sense, would claim that Kipling was the only writer of short stories in English who could be considered the equal of Maupassant and Chekhov. Moreover, Maugham knew from experience 'that 20 years after Kipling wrote his first important stories there were men scattered about the outlying parts of the empire who would never have been just what they were except for him. He not only created characters; he moulded men.' Hemingway would do the same for a generation of Americans, though the laconic, hard-drinking type he created has now, like Kipling's empire-builders, faded away, 'one with Nineveh and Tyre'.

Now that the political questions with which Kipling concerned himself are all in the past, it shouldn't be difficult for us to set aside the animosities he aroused and acknowledge his genius, conceding indeed that the Nobel judges got it right in 1907 — something they haven't done all that often, other English-language winners of the prize including Shaw, Galsworthy, Pearl S. Buck, Churchill, Golding, Bellow and Nadine Gordimer. There are times it has seemed a prize for good conduct rather than literature. Even so a certain prejudice against Kipling survives. *The Oxford Companion to English Literature*, edited by Margaret Drabble, devotes only one column to him, half the space allotted to E. M. Forster. This is absurd.

Part of Kipling's fascination rests in the contradictions he contained. The short-story writer who learned to pare his stories to the bone, cutting them at each of his two or three revisions, seems to have thrown off poems in an often slapdash manner. The 'vulgar jingo' who disgusted sensitive spirits adored France as the fount of civilisation. The bruised and frightened — or, as we should now say, abused — child of *Baa, Baa, Black Sheep* was drawn to cruelty, even sadism — think of the 'cock-fighting' story in *Stalky and Co.*

None of his biographers accepts the late Martin Seymour-Smith's suggestion that he was a repressed homosexual; and yet there are evident homo-erotic and pederastic strains in his work, while in that strangely reticent memoir, *Something of Myself*, he suggested that we all have feelings and impulses it is better not to examine too closely. His art — in *Kim*, *The Jungle Book*, some 40 of the short stories and much of the poetry — offers immediate and unquestioned delight; but his gnomic genius, being timeless can still disturb. These lines, from *The Islanders*, for instance: 'Ancient, effortless, ordered, cycle on cycle set,/ Life so long untroubled, that ye who inherit forget/ It was not made with the mountains, it is not one with the deep./Men, not gods , devised it. Men, not gods, must keep.' Isn't this to the point today?

Yet we might also remember that he liked to quote an Urdu saying, 'Where there are Muslims there is a comprehensible civilisation.'

THE DOUBLE NATURE OF ROMANCE

17 FEBRUARY 2007

The word 'romance' has come down in the world, and the romantic novel is one in which the love-interest predominates. A romance used to be more spirited, a tale of adventure in which the events are striking and come perilously close to being improbable. That scene in my favourite Dumas novel, *Le Vicomte de Bragelonne*, in which d'Artagnan kidnaps General Monck, puts him in a box and transports him across the sea to meet the exiled Charles II and be persuaded to restore him to the throne, is highly improbable but a splendid invention. Dumas is the master of this sort of thing. In *Twenty Years After*, there is another astonishing scene, that in which d'Artagnan and the other musketeers engage to rescue Charles I from the scaffold; they are concealed beneath it, but something — I forget what — has gone wrong; the execution is done and the king's blood drips down on them. Marvellous.

But romance is out of fashion. Most modern thrillers, though full doubtless of exciting incident, lack the sparkle and humanity that characterise the true romance. They tend to be smaller than life, no matter how extravagant the action. Too often also they lack a sense of place, even when the author has conscientiously stuck to the map. One exception was James Buchan's novel set in Persia just before and in the early years of the Iranian Revolution. It was called *A Good Place to Die* and was written with the vivacity that romance demands.

Stevenson, in an interesting and horribly titled essay, *A Gossip on Romance*, declared, 'Drama is the poetry of conduct, romance the poetry of circumstance.' Most serious literary novels are in this sense dramatic. Conduct, how the characters behave, or should behave, to each other is the point of interest.

Such a novel can dispense with striking incident. Nothing much happens in *Emma*, but everything that does happen is significant. Even when, occasionally, Jane Austen does introduce such an incident, the elopement in *Pride and Prejudice*, for instance, she chooses to make nothing of it as such. What concerns her is how her other characters respond to it. Her novels are dramatic in the sense that, as Stevenson puts it in that essay, 'serious theatre exists solely on moral grounds'.

In a romance, however, the hero is caught up in circumstance. Events outside his control force action on him. He may be the victim of the malice of others or of some impersonal fate. It doesn't matter. He must extricate himself as best he can. Romance demands incident, the more striking and exciting the better. The story — there need not be a plot, but there must be a story — moves rapidly. 'The interest turns,' Stevenson suggests, 'not upon what a man may choose to do, but on how he manages to do it.' Not on what he may choose to do, one might add, simply because the freedom of choice is denied him. Circumstance has determined that. At the same time the author of a romance knows that the story must from time to time pause; there must be a modulation of pace, moments of stillness.

The difference between the dramatic novel and the romance is easier to recognise than to define, because one mode may slide into the other; *Great Expectations* is an example of this happening. The opening scene of Pip and the escaped convict on the marshes is pure romance, 'the poetry of circumstance'; the relationship of Pip and Estella is dramatic, 'the poetry of conduct'. The greatest novelists may offer us both in the same book, though, like Jane Austen on one hand and Dumas on the other, they may choose not to. Kipling married drama and romance in many of his short stories, though *The Man who would be King* is marvellous romance. So is *Kim*.

If romance is on my mind, it's because I have just been correcting the proofs of my latest novel. It's called *Charlemagne and Roland* and will be subtitled, defiantly, *A Romance*. The action veers towards the improbable, often, as the characters are, to quote Stevenson again, 'lifted up by circumstance, as by a breaking wave, and dashed we know not how into the future'. At the moment I think it's splendid, marvellously well done, exciting, witty and moving, 'almost in the *Marmion* class,' as Hardy said of *The Iliad*. But, alas, I often think that of my books — at proof stage. It's when they are published that I take a scunner at them and am conscious of how they have failed to be half as good as I dreamed they would be.

FIRST PERSON SINGULAR

3 MARCH 2007

The young Evelyn Waugh, it's said, once declared in a newspaper article that the writing of novels in the first person was a contemptible practice. One would like to think he gave his reasons, but, according to Somerset Maugham, 'he threw out the statement with just the same take-it-or-leave-it casualness as Euclid used when he made his celebrated observation about parallel straight lines.' Subsequently Waugh would write his most popular novel, *Brideshead Revisited*, in that despicable first person. It would have been a poorer novel if he hadn't shown the glamorous Flyte family through the eyes of his narrator, dazzled (if also dull) Charles Ryder. Few readers, I suppose, care much about Ryder's own story, even though it is integral to Waugh's theme — 'the operation of divine grace on a group of diverse but closely connected characters'. Yet it is Ryder's tone of voice, or rather the modulations of that tone, now nostalgic, now enraptured, now weary, now bitter, finally reconciled, that give the novel its peculiar, and for so many of us irresistible, flavour.

Telling your story in the first person has obvious advantages. You engage the reader's interest and sympathy straightaway. This is why so many writers of thrillers or novels of adventure — Stevenson, Buchan, Dick Francis, for example — adopt this mode of telling. The hero-narrator is instantly credible. 'That evening, I remember, as I came up through the Mill Meadow, I was feeling peculiarly happy and contented.' This is how, in the most ordinary way, Buchan has Richard Hannay embark on the wildly improbable story of *The Three Hostages*, and we sense immediately that his happiness and contentment are to be disrupted. The first-person narrative is a means of making the extraordinary acceptable and believable. You have only to compare almost any of Dick Francis's novels, even the weaker among them, with some of his short stories written in the third person to see how speaking in the first person grants authority to the tale.

It's also a reassuring mode. We know that the hero-narrator must survive his ordeal, even when the author doesn't pretend to be giving us a document written by his hero, or to have him telling us the story as he sits by the fire. In theory the novel might end with a sentence that calls his survival into question. Something like this, for instance: 'He smiled as he raised the gun and said, "so, Englishman, you are not so smart as you think you are".' But we should feel cheated.

Graham Greene turned to the first person narrative for *The End of the Affair* after reading *Great Expectations* and being 'captivated by the apparent ease with which Dickens used the first person'. There was an 'obvious technical advantage — the chosen point of view was insured against any temptation to deviate. "I" could only observe what "I" observed (though Proust cheated shamelessly).' He encountered difficulties: 'How could I vary the all-important "tone" when it was one character who was always commenting?' He 'dreaded to see the whole book smoked dry like a fish with his [the narrator's] hatred'. Nevertheless that novel, and *The Quiet American* in which he also told the story in the first person, seem to me two of Greene's most assured successes.

The method has another merit, more evident perhaps to novelists as they grow older, especially to those trying to write what are styled, annoyingly but inescapably, literary novels. You don't have to claim more knowledge of other people than you actually possess. Young authors may pretend to omniscience, but with age we come to realise how little or how imperfectly we ever know even those close to us, how ignorant we are of what goes on in their minds. Our knowledge is at best partial, derived only from how they display themselves. Everything beyond that is mere guesswork. The temptation to play God with the characters we have brought into being weakens. At the same time the writer's imagination usually becomes duller. Moreover, since writing is a solitary business, the novelist sees less of other people than he used to. In any case we all know that the sort of relationships we enjoyed in youth are behind us; we no longer 'tire the sun with talking, and send him down the sky'.

'The pleasant voices, the nightingales' live only in a fading memory. But we remain bound to the wheel; we have to go on making novels. One recourse is to retreat into history or fantasy; another, and perhaps more worthwhile one, is to write from one's own experience, necessarily limited as we now recognise it to be; to employ the first-person narrator who confessedly writes of other people from outside, creating characters from how they show themselves, but no longer pretending to know what goes on in their mind. In short, using the first person allows us to present other people as they must be: that is, ultimately mysterious beings.

THE TRUE AND
THE CREDIBLE

17 MARCH 2007

Some 20 years ago A. N. Wilson published a novel entitled *Gentlemen in England*. It was savagely reviewed in *The Spectator* by the late Lord Lambton. He complained that two characters were portraits of old friends of his, whom, for the purpose of the review, he called Mr F. and Mr Q. (Alastair Forbes and Peter Quennell, one guessed, without much difficulty.) Quoting a snatch of dialogue, he declared that Mr F. (or it may have been Mr Q.) would never have said such a thing, and therefore the whole edifice fell flat. This prompted me to write a letter pointing out that since Mr Wilson had written a novel in which neither Mr F. not Mr Q. was a character, how either would have spoken in real life was utterly irrelevant.

I remembered this when reading William Waldegrave's review of Justin Cartwright's novel *The Song Before it is Sung*. Unlike Lambton's it wasn't a hatchet job. Indeed it was for the most part admiring. Nevertheless some of the criticisms Lord Waldegrave offered seemed to me to arise from the same sort of misunderstanding of the difference between fiction and what for want of a better term one must call 'real life'.

Few readers with any knowledge of the 1930s and of the aristocratic German opposition to Hitler will fail to realise, only a few pages into the novel, that the two principal characters are modelled on Sir Isaiah Berlin and Adam zu Solz von Trott; and indeed Cartwright adds an 'Afterword' in which he says that 'the story is based in part on the friendship between' them. Nevertheless this is a work of fiction and Elya Mendel and Axel von Gottberg are distanced from their originals. This permits the author a freedom which he would not have enjoyed to the same extent had he chosen to call his characters Berlin and Trott. At least he would have been denied that freedom if he had a scrupulous regard for the facts of biography and history.

Waldegrave was disturbed by 'the novel's proposition', that Berlin's 'repudiation' of Trott meant that he had 'some moral responsibility for von Trott's horrible and heroic death'. Since Waldegrave was, I think, a friend of Sir Isaiah, both being also Fellows of All Souls, his distress is understandable. It does credit to his heart. But it is not relevant to a reading of the novel, which will after all be read and judged by many who know little or nothing of Berlin and Trott. For them the question will be whether Cartwright has made his fiction convincing.

Since Waldegrave is an intelligent and judicious critic, he realises this himself, asking whether we shouldn't be judging Cartwright not on his portrayal of the real-life friendship between Berlin and Trott, but 'against the criteria we use when we read pure fiction sparked by real events, fiction which creates a world to be judged on its own terms, a world like that of Stendhal or Scott'. The answer is surely 'yes, these are the criteria we should employ'.

The questions how you may introduce real-life characters into a novel, and do so credibly and with propriety, are not easy to answer — even less so today when we so often see actors impersonating politicians and members of the royal family in films and television programmes. Nevertheless, there is perhaps one useful guideline: the more distant in time, the more liberties the novelist may fairly take. If, however, you wish to introduce recent historical figures into a novel, then it is best to have them seen through the eyes of fictional characters. In this way you set them at a distance. They are presented to the reader as they present themselves to characters of the author's devising. There is no pretence that you are giving the 'real Churchill or de Gaulle', for example; only Churchill or de Gaulle as he might have seemed to an invented character. This aids credibility because it effectively makes them part of a fiction. You are not pretending to enter their minds because even when you have them speak or act, their words or deeds are filtered to the reader by way of the consciousness of an imagined observer.

If you don't choose this method, then it is wise to do as Cartwright has done: take them away from the real-life model by giving them other names and thus being free to invent conversations, acts and episodes at will. In any case, real life is too complicated for the novel, too discordant. The novelist is selective; real life is, as Stevenson wrote, 'monstrous, infinite, illogical', too much altogether. The novelist draws on life by means of observation and experience, which is memory; but he illuminates it by his imagination. His characters may resemble people in real life, but, unlike them, they are composed of only a few thousand words.

ANGUS WILSON
TAKING RISKS

31 MARCH 2007

Auden, discussing *Troilus and Cressida*, remarked that major writers set themselves new challenges, and so risk failure, while minor ones are content to do the same thing as before and so risk nothing. There's something in this, though, like many of his pronouncements, it's too sweeping to be altogether true. (Besides which, the major/minor categorisation is tiresome, even if we all resort to it from time to time.)

Instead of indulging in the sheep-and-goats of major/minor, it may simply be that some writers become bored with what they have done, or fear becoming what Graham Greene called 'prisoners of their method', and so strike out on a new line; plenty of bad writers after all set themselves new and different challenges, even if they fail to meet them. Others, good and bad alike, are content to refine their method, rework their material. In any case novelty doesn't require a marked shift in tone or content. Shakespeare has a scope denied to Racine, but Racine is capable of a more intense concentration of effect.

This is a diversion or distraction — something Shakespeare allowed himself often, Racine never — because really I wanted to talk about Angus Wilson, who on this matter agreed with Auden. In an affectionate essay Rose Tremain wrote that Wilson taught her 'to take risks, to resist petrifaction, to try to chart in each book new territory, to be sceptical about what one has achieved so far'.

He wrote only eight novels himself, and in each he set himself a new challenge, explored new territory, leaving far behind the material and manner of the excellent short stories with which he made his name. The stories themselves remain to my mind wonderfully good; nobody catches so precisely the post-war world of the shabby-genteel where dubious majors pass dodgy cheques. One assumes Wilson could have continued in this vein.

Of the novels, the last two, *As if by Magic* and *Setting the World on Fire*, seem to me duds, and I don't care for *The Middle Age of Mrs Eliot*; it's well done, and the portrait of Mrs Eliot forced to re-order her life after the sudden death of her husband is good — she exhibits that 'pluck' which Wilson admired in women, admired too, if reluctantly, in his majors keeping up appearances as best they can in their threadbare tweed suits. (They all owe something to his father.)

But the other five novels are a remarkable body of work, books which bear frequent re-reading. The first, *Hemlock and After*, is still somewhat in the manner of the short stories, and very funny, as well as wise and painful. *Anglo-Saxon Attitudes* is more ambitious, with a complicated nineteenth-century plot; it has a huge range of characters, including one of his finest grotesques, and covers some four decades with masterful ease. It has also some of his finest set-pieces, one notably ghastly party.

In one sense it points towards his sixth novel, *No Laughing Matter*, which is a sort of family saga, witty, imaginative, compassionate, highly intelligent, full of characters whose vitality is astonishing. In between are two utterly different novels. *The Old Men at the Zoo*, published in 1961, is ostensibly about a war between Britain and the European Union sometime in the 1970s. It was received with some uncertainty by most reviewers. Evelyn Waugh, who had admired Wilson's work from the start, was sufficiently 'dismayed' by its reception to write a reproving letter to *The Spectator*, praising the 'technical achievement of its intricate structure' and saying he had read it 'with keen delight and admiration'. (How splendid, if one had received a bad review, to have Waugh coming chivalrously to one's defence! He also wrote what he described as 'a fan letter' to Wilson.) In his *Spectator* letter he suggested that, consciously or not, Wilson had described not a future war but the invasion that many feared in 1938-40 and its possible consequences.

Wilson's next novel, *Late Call*, explored very different territory. Set in a New Town, it deals with apparently very ordinary people leading unexciting lives. The heroine is an elderly woman, married to an unsatisfactory husband — a relic of the 1914–18 war, a 'temporary gentleman' as the term was. They come in retirement to live with their son, recently widowed trendy headmaster of a comprehensive. Sounds dull? Only to those who don't like novels in which, as Jane Austen put it, 'the most thorough knowledge of human nature, the happiest delineation of its varieties, the liveliest effusions of wit and humour are conveyed to the world in the best chosen language'.

Angus Wilson died in 1991, and his work is now out of fashion. I can't believe it will remain so. If it does, the worse for readers in the future.

NOT CONTENT WITH
THE CONTENTS

14 APRIL 2007

Degas once complained to Mallarmé that he had been trying to write a sonnet, unsuccessfully, though he had had such a good idea for it. 'Alas, my poor Edgar,' was the reply, 'poems are made with words, not with ideas.' A neat comment, but is it always possible to distinguish between the two? Even a 'nonsense poem' is not devoid of ideas: 'The vorpal blade went snicker-snack'. Nonsense words, yet the idea is evident. How to separate aesthetic delight from content?

The question becomes more acute still when you turn to consideration of the novel. Nabokov, better critic than novelist to my mind, went for aesthetic delight, 'the tingle in the spine'. 'Cherish the details,' he said. Fair enough, but there is of necessity more to a good novel than this. Ford Madox Ford, a better critic and novelist than Nabokov, thought that imaginative literature was the greatest of art forms because it could make you think and feel at the same time. This too is doubtless an exaggeration, a piece of special pleading. Can't music and painting do this also?

Theories of aesthetics can restrict painting to an arrangement of shapes and lines, Roger Fry's argument about 'significant form'. Certainly analysis of these matters may account for the delight a painting may offer us. Yet, for most of the history of European art, painters have been equally concerned with content. What is the point of making a painting of some story or scene from classical mythology if the idea of what is represented is not intended to make an impression on us?

NOT CONTENT WITH THE CONTENTS

There is in any case more than one way in which we may properly respond to a work of art. William Empson, for instance, wrote in *Milton's God* that 'the essential function of imaginative literature is to make you realise that other people act on moral convictions different from your own'. This is some way from Nabokov's assertion that 'great novels are great fairy tales', though of course they may be that too.

Nabokov despised what he called 'the matter-of-fact reader' who might suppose that the chief interest of *À La Recherche du Temps Perdu* lies in Proust's exploration of the social world and so 'will probably conclude that the main action of the book consists of a series of parties'. We may agree that this poor fellow is missing rather a lot, missing indeed the essential meaning of the work (if indeed it has such an identifiable meaning, something we may dispute). Nevertheless he surely has a point. Much of the pleasure of the novel is indeed to be found in these social passages, which evidently mattered to Proust as they do to the 'matter-of-fact reader'. Otherwise he wouldn't have spent so much time and effort elaborating them, enjoying himself no end, one supposes, as he did so. Indeed, while Proust does provide, time and again, that 'tingle in the spine' that Nabokov demands, he also abundantly satisfies Empson's requirement, making us realise that 'other people act on moral convictions different from our own'. In doing so he enlarges and deepens our understanding of life. And this is something the great writer always does.

He does this by opening a new window on experience. A merely competent novelist reproduces the world, so that, in reading his book, we find ourselves saying 'yes, that's true to life, that's how it is'; and this is indeed no mean achievement, one that many fail to bring off. But the great writer does more than this. He lets us see the world in a new and distinctive light. Instead of saying 'that's true to experience', we look at the world around us, at society, at habits of thought, speech and action, and say, 'but that's pure Dickens or Dostoevsky, Proust or Stendhal, Waugh or Greene'. He pulls back a curtain and shows us something we have never seen before.

But to do this successfully the novelist must also do much else, and a good deal of this will not offer aesthetic delight, will pull back no curtain, but will indeed quite often be rather flat. I open, for example, *David Copperfield* at random and happen on a paragraph about Mr Spenlow's failure to make a will. It's written in that easy conversational tone of which Dickens was by then a master and so is pleasing, but its purpose is to convey necessary information, no more than that. Yet any novel must contain many such passages.

The details of a novel are cherishable, the structure must satisfy, and the tone give delight, but because a novel is a narrative peopled with characters whose actions are the consequence of what they feel and what they think, every novelist is as concerned with content as with manner, with what as well as how. And inevitably much in any long narrative will be merely workmanlike, tingling no spines.

IS HILAIRE BELLOC
OUT OF DATE?

28 APRIL 2007

A. N. Wilson, in his admirable biography, concluded that Belloc
was more remarkable as a man than in his writings. No doubt he
was, and his case is not unusual. The same has been said often
of Dr Johnson and of Byron, while I know people who return
frequently to Walter Scott's Journal, fascinated by the man who
presents himself there, but who never open any of the Waverley
novels. Likewise Hemingway and Fitzgerald have now been the
subjects of more biographies and memoirs than the sum total of
the books they themselves wrote, evidence at least of the magnetic
influence of their personalities. Of course there are those of whom
the opposite is true: Shakespeare obviously, perhaps Proust, despite
all that has been written about the man; Wodehouse certainly. But
it is clear that interest in some writers may persist while their works
gather dust or are almost all out of print. Even so, it's unlikely we
would know anything about them if they hadn't first been admired
for what they wrote. If Johnson hadn't been a celebrity, Boswell
would not have been attracted to him.

A great deal of Belloc's work is dead, even deservedly dead. Few,
perhaps nobody, will now read the four volumes of his *History of
England* or the historical biographies he churned out, repetitiously,
in the 1920s and 30s. They all make the same argument, challenging
the Protestant or Whig interpretation of English history. For one
thing, even if these books were better than they are, the argument is
no longer necessary. Much of what Belloc had to say about the class
basis of the Reformation and the nature of the Catholic resistance

to this revolution has since been said, more authoritatively, by academic historians.

He wrote too much because he was always hard pressed for money, which is a characteristic of literary men, and no good at managing it, which is another. And, because he wrote too much, he sometimes wrote badly, and when he had nothing to say, or nothing that he hadn't said a hundred times before, he would disguise this by raising his voice and shouting; which is also quite common, as anyone who has written a 'why, oh why?' piece can tell you. The less we have to say, or the less original the message, the more vigorously we pound the pulpit to which we have been assigned.

What then survives? The *Cautionary Tales* certainly; they still delight intelligent children; adults too, for many lines come often, unbidden, to one's mind.

The serious poetry hasn't dated, perhaps because it was old-fashioned in style and tone when he wrote it. Belloc was no modernist, his manner classical. Then there is *The Modern Traveller*, a masterpiece of light verse; 'The nuisance of the Tropics is/ The sheer necessity of fizz.' Kipling was his only contemporary rival as writer of verse epigrams. 'Thus, richly, with ridiculous display,/ The politician's corpse was laid away./ While all of his acquaintance sneered and slanged,/ I wept, for I had longed to see him hanged.' Few have done scorn better than Belloc.

In prose, despite fine set-pieces in the early historical works, the battle scenes being especially vivid, his best work is to be found in his essays. Even his most satisfactory full-length books, like *The Path to Rome*, are really made up of essays loosely strung together. I prefer his essays to Chesterton's; they are less wearing and more varied in tone and manner. In the little book before me there is one entitled *On Irony*; it is grave and wise. The word itself has become debased, was indeed so when Belloc wrote, Fowler in MEU protesting against

74

'the application of "irony" to every trivial oddity'. How much more so today when the words 'ironical' and 'ironically' are over-used, vaguely used, and effectively divested of meaning. Belloc's essay is Johnsonian, a reminder that he thought *Rasselas* a book that one should read every year, and superior to *Candide*, perhaps because its irony is more sombre.

But what of this, which seems to me wonderfully good?

> There comes a time in the moral disruption of a State when the mere utterance of a plain truth, laboriously concealed by hypocrisy, denied by contemporary falsehood and forgotten in the moral lethargy of the populace, takes upon itself an ironical quality more powerful than any elaboration of special ironies could have taken in the past … In such awful moments in the history of a State that which makes the dreadful jest is not the jester, but the eternal principle of truth itself.

Belloc out of date? Surely not. Isn't this a statement of the necessary role of irony in our own day, when public discourse is rich in hypocrisy and downright falsehood and judgment is corrupted by that moral lethargy of which he speaks?

WHEN THE GOING
WAS BETTER

12 MAY 2007

In January 1923 Aldous Huxley signed a contract with Chatto & Windus, which would guarantee him a regular income for three years. He would be paid £500 per annum and in return agreed to 'supply the publishers with two new works of fiction a year, one of them to be a full-length novel'—an onerous undertaking. The royalty rate was to start at 15 per cent, rising to 20 per cent after the first 2,000 copies sold, and to 25 per cent after 8,000. This contract was regularly renewed over the years, with some emendations (one non-fiction book being substituted for one of the works of fiction) while by the second or third renewal the initial royalty rate would rise to 20 per cent. Novelists today can only be envious. Huxley enjoyed a high reputation, but he was never a bestseller like Hugh Walpole or Somerset Maugham, to say nothing of genre writers such as Edgar Wallace, Agatha Christie, Dennis Wheatley and Peter Cheyney. Perhaps some bestsellers today can demand and get comparable royalty rates, but the average literary novelist who is well-reviewed but sells only respectably certainly can't look for such generosity from his publishers.

Since publishers who wish to stay in business are rarely philanthropists, one may ask how Chatto managed to offer such high royalties. After all, the advance they were offering was quite high — and would indeed rise to more than £1,000 a year later. First, of course, they were demanding a lot from Huxley himself, but this is an inadequate answer. Few novelists today are likely to be offered a starting royalty of more than 10 per cent, while paperback royalties may start as low as 7.5 per cent.

One explanation is that publishing was itself a very different business then, with much lower overheads than now. Publishers didn't occupy expensive premises. Their offices were often small, shabby and pokey. (This was still the case even in the 1970s when I was first published by The Bodley Head; you nodded to a porter in his cubby-hole and mounted a rickety wooden stair to see your editor.) They had far fewer staff. Evelyn Waugh remembered that his father, as managing director of Chapman & Hall, 'interviewed all authors, artists, printers, binders, and himself drew up advertisements. He communicated with other parts of the office by whistling down a tube for the office boy ... and he handled alone all the work that is now performed by four or five executives.'

Secondly, there was a guaranteed sale to public libraries. I don't know how large this was between the wars, but in the Fifties and Sixties it might come to some 2,000 copies. By the late Seventies this was down to 750. What is it today — if, indeed, there is any such guaranteed sale?

Thirdly, the Net Book Agreement protected prices, and, partly in consequence, booksellers were less powerful and less grasping than they are now. The regular discounting of the published price to the booksellers was 33 per cent; 40 per cent was exceptional even 30 or 40 years after Huxley signed that contract. Today the chains that dominate the book trade can demand and get 50 per cent, sometimes even 55. The balance has swung in their favour, and both publishers and authors have suffered as a result. We have arrived at the remarkable position in which the party who does least (the bookseller) gets most, five times as much of the recommended cover price of a novel as the author who brought it into being, and almost twice as much as the publisher who bore all the costs of production.

Finally the shelf-life of a new hardback is much shorter than it used to be, as little as six weeks. After that time the returns flood back to the publisher, and months later these copies appear as minus sales on the royalty statement to depress the author who has probably been told happily by the publicity girl when the book came out that 'the subscription is good'.

No wonder a novelist today may look enviously on Huxley's contracts, all the more so because his assured income from Chatto & Windus enabled him and his wife Maria to live in some style in Italy and France, and even in 1929 buy and run what Huxley described as 'the new touring model of the Bugatti which has a most extraordinary performance and is a very sound piece of engineering and building'. Admittedly Huxley worked very hard — when he worked — writing, for instance, the 100,000 words of *Antic Hay* in two months; but between books their existence, as described by his biographer Sybille Bedford, sounds idyllic.

Things are different today. They were different even 20 years ago. As Anthony Burgess once said to me (and doubtless to many others as well), 'we used to live on royalties, now we live on advances' — and even they are harder to come by, and less generous for the middle-ranking literary novelist, than they were. 'O Tempora, O Mores', he may sigh in melancholy mood.

ORDERING THE STEPS
OF THE DANCE…

26 MAY 2007

Writing a novel is a voyage into unknown territory. (Reading one is also, of course.) The author explores possibilities. To some extent even those novels which seem far removed from autobiography represent the author's imaginary, or alternative, life, characters owing more in the last resort to him than to any identifiable models. He is a puppet-master, ordering the steps of the dance. Nevertheless he is likely, in the writing, often to be taken by surprise. 'How do I know what I mean till I see what I've said?' What to the reader seems right, even inevitable, might have taken a different course.

The truth of this is well illustrated by the jottings Anthony Powell made, published posthumously as *A Writer's Notebook*. Though rich in nice observation — 'A great deal of individual success in life is based on not having the slightest idea what other people are like' — their chief interest for those addicted to his great work are the glimpses they offer of what went into the making of it. Sometimes you have the first draft of a comment, not yet attributed to any character: 'The really extraordinary thing about professional seducers is the drivel they talk, there is not a single cliché they leave unsaid. That is why they have such success with women.' This line will later be given to Maclintick in *Casanova's Chinese Restaurant*. Others were never used: 'Poets as a class are so hard on whisky.' You find ideas which turn out to have been false starts: 'The Army Book should begin with something fairly grim like a suicide.' It doesn't: the two suicides come later.

Characters, the reader will realise, are formed tentatively in the author's mind. 'Erridge is killed in the Spanish War, his younger brother in the '39-45 war, and they have to sell the house.' '? Erridge ? Gypsy Jones. Against the war at the start, in favour when Russia comes in, later anti-atom plant.' 'Possibly in the end Erridge marries Gypsy Jones . . . ' In fact, as we know, Erridge never marries, while Gypsy turns up at his funeral, now married to Howard Craggs, the left-wing publisher. From such notes one learns that an author may have a clear idea of a character, yet be uncertain what to do with him.

When did Powell decide that Widmerpool should join Scorpio Mortlock's cult? Quite late, I surmise. So we have: 'Widmerpool says at the end, "I have had a happy life on the whole, I think I can say people have liked me."' This strikes a false note, so wasn't used. But clearly he was puzzled as to how best to finish with his monster: '? Widmerpool dies in a hi-jacked plane.' No, unsatisfactory: try again.

There are interesting reflections on his art. 'One of the difficulties of writing a novel is that in real life a million small things bring about some situation, which has usually to be represented as the result of one big thing in a book.' This chimes with Stevenson's remark about real life being too diffuse for art. The novelist works by means of selection, and the success of a novel depends on making the most plausible or convincing choice. This doesn't exclude improbability, for life offers us examples of this every day. Compare what V. S. Pritchett said was the starting-point of some of his stories: the question provoked by a couple in a bar or restaurant, 'what does he see in her?' The novelist's problem is then how to make the apparently improbable convincing. Why, for instance, does Jean Templer go to bed with her ex-brother- in-law Jimmy Stribling and the appalling Jimmy Brent? Nick Jenkins can't understand it. Powell enables the reader to do so. Yet one is left with the question Nick might have

asked himself: 'If her taste runs to Bob Duport and the two Jimmys
— what does that make me?'

Powell's notebook also confirms a truth that all novelists must
be acquainted with, one that is however apparently concealed
from many critics: that in making a novel the writer is concerned
above all not with ideas, themes, symbols — all of which emerge
unconsciously and which he himself may not even be aware of till
the book is finished — but rather with severely practical questions.
What does X do now? What on earth are these people to say to
each other now that I have got them together? And finally the
novelist comes to realise another truth: 'Everyone is at least three
people, what they are, what they think they are, what the world
thinks they are.' It is his task at least to hint at the first of these
— 'what they are' — while nevertheless showing that the person
himself and those around him remain ignorant of this.

Which is why good novels make more sense of life than life
itself manages to do.

PARADISE BEFORE THE GUNS OPENED FIRE

9 JUNE 2007

Reviewing recently a new English version of Alain-Fournier's 1913 novel *Le Grand Meaulnes*, I was happy and relieved to find that it retains its magic. It has entranced generations of adolescents, not all of them French, but I had wondered if it would still appeal after so many years. It is an extraordinary book, part fairytale or romance, part realistic study of French provincial life, sometimes grim, in the last years of the nineteenth century; and some of its fascination comes from this curiously hybrid quality. It is both naive and knowing. It has the dewy freshness of a first novel, but it is also admirably constructed, reminding one that Alain-Fournier, though only 26 when the novel appeared, was no provincial innocent, but already belonged to the literary establishment. His closest friend (and brother-in-law) Jacques Rivière became editor of the *Nouvelle Revue Française*, and Alain-Fournier himself knew Gide and his circle.

Part of its attraction for us is doubtless the picture it presents of rural France before it had felt any of the shock of modernity. Yet it is Meaulnes's discovery of 'the lost estate' (the title given to this new translation) and his attempt to find his way back to this briefly-experienced paradise — this glimpse of Eden — that gives the novel its peculiar and enduring charm, and it struck me on this reading that, thoroughly and engagingly French as it is, it belongs very much to its period. The main action may be set in the 1890s, but the atmosphere is also that of the golden Edwardian afternoon.

One finds the same sort of feeling in much that was written this side of the Channel, even, for example, *The Wind in the Willows*. The chapter entitled 'The Piper at the Gates of Dawn' and that one in which Mole is lost and terrified in the Wild Wood, have the same other-worldly atmosphere.Kipling offers it too in *Puck of Pook's Hill* and *Rewards and Fairies*, while, wholly different in setting and narrative as it may be, his masterpiece Kim resembles *Le Grand Meaulnes* in its suggestion that the truths perceived in childhood and adolescence have a vivid reality deriving from the sense of wonder which will grow dim with the passing of the years. Moreover Kim, like Meaulnes, is uncertain of his identity: 'Who is Kim — Kim — Kim?' he asks. And then there is Peter Pan.

But perhaps the Edwardian writer whose work at times most evidently breathes the same spirit as Alain-Fournier's is Saki, in stories such as *The Music on the Hill* and *The Hounds of Fate*:

> Stonor heard his adopted name called in a tone of strained anxiety. Instantly he knew that something untoward had happened, and with a quick revulsion of outlook his sanctuary became in his eyes a place of peace and contentment, from which he dreaded to be driven.

As with Alain-Fournier, Saki suggests that 'reality' — the truth about things — is there, only to be glimpsed, the other side of a veil; that there is an Eden which we may visit in youth but from which we must be expelled in later years.

Describing Signorelli's painting *The Triumph of Pan*, the Franco-American writer Julien Green (born 1900) found that:

> A shadow hung over these enigmatic festivities. Such a look of languor on the face of Pan detached him from paganism. If he ruled over these bodies, he did so in the late afternoon light; the mood was joyful, but dusk was approaching.

If this seems to catch the atmosphere of that time, catch indeed something of the mood of *Le Grand Meaulnes*, it is no doubt in part because of our awareness now of how that world was to be shattered by the guns that opened fire in August 1914, after which it was no longer possible to believe in Eden — or indeed in Pan or Puck; still less in any innocence.

Writing in 1947 an introduction to Saki's novel, *The Unbearable Bassington*, Evelyn Waugh found it 'impossible in reading [it] . . . at this date to avoid a prophetic and allegorical interpretation which cannot have been consciously present to the author. It was 1912. 'Comus' — an Arcadian name, one may note — 'had only to wait two years to find full employment for his talents. He was cannon-fodder in a time of peace.' Saki himself was killed in the trenches in November 1916. Alain-Fournier went earlier, in the first weeks of the war. One can't doubt that Le Grand Meaulnes himself died at the Marne or Verdun. Between 1914 and 1918 the paradisal lost estate was lost. The wind no longer blew through the willows and Pook's Hill was deserted. 'To die,' said Peter, 'will be an awfully big adventure.' It became the common experience of millions of young men, and their successors; those whom Gertrude Stein called 'the lost generation' were exiled from Alain-Fournier's lost estate. Only the magic of art — his art and that of others — enables us to imagine it.

THE PHANTOMS OF
THE OPERA

23 JUNE 2007

No doubt Mr Blair will soon be at work on his memoirs; or perhaps his ghost will. Ghosts play a necessary role in the publishing business. Indeed all those firms who rely for their profits on the autobiographies — and even occasionally the novels — of celebrities might collapse without the work of these industrious spectres. Till quite recently their existence was veiled in obscurity and the pretence was maintained that politicians, actors, singers and sportspersons were indeed the authors of the books which appeared under their name. This make-believe is no longer sustainable. Too many so-called authors have casually remarked in interviews that they haven't actually read their own book. (No politician has yet been honest enough to make this admission. 'What's new?' you say.) Now ghosts are recognised. We all know that Hunter Davies has been slaving away at the five-volume autobiography of Wayne Rooney. Uphill work, indeed; Churchill's War Memoirs ran to six volumes with some ghostly assistance, but his was a rather fuller life than the young Manchester United striker's.

There is nothing new in the use of ghosts. Dumas for instance employed them to make drafts of novels or write those passages that bored him. In nineteenth-century France ghosts were known as *nègres*; suitably enough, since negritude then still connoted slavery. I doubt if the term is now permissible, though such is the admirable conservatism of France that it may yet be employed, if only surreptitiously. Dumas used ghosts to save time and enable him to meet all his commitments. Other novelists have done so, reluctantly, because their talent was exhausted. Francis King revealed in his autobiography, *Yesterday Came Suddenly*, that he had ghosted substantial parts of some of L. P. Hartley's last books.

The greatest of ghost-masters was Colette's first husband, the extraordinary Willy. Starting out as a poet (bad career choice), he became a literary capitalist, an entrepreneur of letters who would supply columns, essays, paragraphs of gossip, dialogues and eventually novels, books of scandalous history and spurious memoirs; and of these he would write scarcely a line himself. Colette's Claudine novels were first published under her husband's name. Most of his other poor ghosts are now forgotten, except perhaps for Marcel Boulestin, restaurateur and author (under his own name) of cookery books. The ghosts were driven hard. In *Mes Apprentissages* Colette wrote, 'Whenever we veterans of the old gang meet and talk of our duped and despoiled past, we always say, "in the days when we worked in the factory".' Willy himself developed an utter aversion to writing. Yet his case was not that 'of an ordinary man who engaged other men to write the books he signed', for 'the man who did not write was more talented than the men who wrote in his stead'. Not so with our modern celebrity authors. The other remarkable feature of Willy's factory was that he gave his ghosts the most detailed, copious and intelligent instructions and subjected their work to close criticism, before perhaps passing it to some other spectre to revise. He often spent more time cajoling work from others and indicating how it must be revised than would have been necessary for him to do himself. But that was just what he found beyond him. Later Colette attributed this inability to 'an undeniable condition of morbid laziness and a timidity of expression'. But I suspect he enjoyed the pleasures of intrigue and found the organisation of his factory of ghosts more rewarding, not only financially.

Colette escaped the factory to become an author in her own right whose fame and achievement far surpassed Willy's; his most successful ghost put on flesh. If we are to believe the Baconians or (if you prefer) the Oxfordians, the man of Stratford pulled off the most remarkable of coups in the world of spectral authorship. Hired to put his name to the plays that Bacon (or the Earl of Oxford) wrote, he convinced all but the most alert detector of conspiracies that he was indeed their author. This, if true and not a flight of fancy from the wilder shores of lunacy, would be an extraordinary inversion of ghostly relationships. Believe it if you must, though to my mind if you can suppose Bacon (or Oxford) to have written the plays ascribed to Shakespeare, you ought to be able to picture Wayne Rooney at typewriter or computer.

Be that as it may, these are good years for ghosts. There can scarcely be a successful publisher who doesn't believe in them. Without the work of ghosts, publishers might not afford their subscriptions to the Garrick, might even, horrible thought, be unable to lunch. 'Old mole,' says the prudent publisher, 'canst work i' the earth so fast as to get the book out in time for the Christmas market?' And if he can't? Then hire a second ghost and a third, till the line stretches on to the crack of doom and the book is done.

'KEEP ALL ON GOOING'

4 AUGUST 2007

Francis King's new novel was published a few weeks ago. Nothing, you may say, remarkable about that. He is among the most professional of authors; writing novels is what he does. Well, yes, of course, but it is certainly worth remarking that his first novel appeared in 1946. A career spanning six decades: not many can match that. What is equally remarkable is that this new novel, *With My Little Eye*, is as fresh, perceptive, lively and moving as anything he has written. Ford Madox Ford, in one of his splendid books of rambling reminiscences, wrote admiringly of an old Kentish countrywoman, Meary, who, near the end of a hard life, used to tell him that the only thing to do is to 'keep all on gooing'. Francis King has certainly done that.

Many can't. They might like to, but other things get in the way. They run out of material or energy. Their imagination flags. They no longer see the world around them as material for fiction. It becomes difficult to concern themselves with the doings of imaginary beings. Few formally give up, though the Who's Who entry of John Heygate (known, I daresay, to many only as the man who broke up Evelyn Waugh's first marriage) used to read, 'Novelist (retired)'. On the other hand some are abandoned by their publishers, and eventually give up hope of finding a replacement. This is perhaps sad, but not surprising. Publishers, like the Athenians (in St Paul's view), are neophiliacs, lusting after something new.

Cyril Connolly listed, in *Enemies of Promise*, the obstacles which might bring a writer down and prevent him from going on. The best remembered of these was 'the pram in the hall' — even in the days when fathers were rarely expected to occupy themselves with their young children. Another was journalism — did he call that something to do with the charlock, a weed which may flourish in fields of wheat and choke its growth? Reporting may be, as Hemingway claimed, good training for a novelist, but writing columns, or editing, or simply being a success in newspapers, may stifle the talent for making fiction, or simply leave neither room nor time for it to be exercised. Did that happen to, for instance, Godfrey Smith, author of a delightful novel of Middle England in the Thirties and Forties, *The Business of Loving*, which appeared in 1961? There were a couple of later novels, but journalism took over. The trade is absorbing, its embrace often crushing. Only a few successfully manage over the years to combine journalism with the writing of good novels, Ferdinand Mount being perhaps the best example in our time.

Often the well from which you draw runs dry. That happened to Simon Raven. As his biographer Michael Barber put it, 'the rich vein of material he had accumulated as a young man was exhausted, and all he could do was recycle the end product'. It is neither surprising nor reprehensible that this should happen; Evelyn Waugh thought that most of us had material for only half a dozen books; 'the rest is professional trickery'. Sometimes you strike it lucky and are given unlooked for new experience; he got this with Pinfold.

The author of the first (brief) review of my own new novel wondered how I see my career. 'He has found himself rather pigeonholed as a writer of historical fiction, and the books on which he honed his skills, contemporary literary fiction . . . have been forgotten.' Sad, no doubt, but there it is. You write what you have the material to write, and that material is supplied partly by imagination, partly by observation, partly by experience, or, if you prefer, memory. Writing historical fiction you draw less heavily on your own experience. The material is there waiting to be used. It's a way to 'keep all on gooing'.

It is easy for novelists to lose touch with the world about them. Writing is a solitary trade, requiring you to live much of the time not only on your own but in your own mind. You may find your curiosity about other people ebb. You may also find yourself less able to enter into their lives, less confident of understanding them. This is one reason why older novelists may, like very young ones, prefer to use a first-person narrator, with no claim to the omniscience they know themselves to lack. Worst of all, they may come to find the world — and other people — rather dull. What is really extraordinary about Francis King is that, after 60 years of writing fiction, his curiosity is as lively as ever. Allied to his masterly craftsmanship, this makes him, even in his eighties, among the freshest and most rewarding of novelists, one to cherish.

FROM SHETLAND
WITH TRUTH

18 AUGUST 2007

A novelist is rarely well-advised to write his masterpiece in his fifties, unless his position at the top of the tree is secure. His themes and style are no longer likely to be in fashion. A younger generation of writers is occupying the attention of reviewers and speaking with greater immediacy to the public. This was Eric Linklater's experience. He had achieved popularity and critical respect in the Thirties with *Juan in America* and his best prewar novel *Magnus Merriman*, and maintained his position after the war with *Private Angelo* and *Laxdale Hall*. But by the mid-1950s, when he wrote *The Dark of Summer*, he was, if not in the wilderness, at least on its fringes.

Yet this is a great novel, beautifully crafted, its themes sombre and important. It deals with war, with the deformation of character which may result from clinging to unhappy memories, with an act of treason, with courage and cowardice and the possibility of redemption through love and, in two instances, self-sacrifice. The second of these, in the Korean war, moves me to tears every time I read the book; it is so brave, so necessary from one point of view, so totally uncalled-for from another.

It's a novel of an extraordinary range. It moves back and forward in time, as far back as to an interpolated section which recounts a squalid sequel to the Jacobite Rising of 1745, through the 1939–45 war and up almost to the time it was written. The setting is various: Shetland, London, the North Sea, the Faroes, the Western Desert, the Italian campaign and the grim battle for Monte Cassino, Korea, Paris. It begins and ends in Shetland and that is where its heart is.

You may think this is a lot of travelling for quite a short novel — little more than 250 pages. A lesser writer might indeed have made a book three or four times as long from such a wealth of material. Yet nothing is skimped, while no scene — and there are some tremendous scenes — is prolonged beyond what is required. It is written with a sharp-cutting economy, like Waugh's *Sword of Honour*.

At the same time it's curiously leisurely. There is no suggestion of haste; there are moments of reflection. The narrator is a professional soldier, and the novel's most ironical sentence is his disclaimer: 'I cannot tell my story as neatly as, I daresay, a professional author would tell it.'

Near the end he has a dream in which he is swimming upstream, and, when he wakes, he reflects on the concept of time which he has always thought of, as I suppose many of us do, as a river. 'But I no longer think of it as a stream flowing from the past. In my dream it ran the other way.' The passage is too long to quote here, but the gist is that 'memories gather about us, but against the current memory can be let go, and the stream will carry it away'. The centrepiece of the novel tells of a man, a Shetland laird, formerly a colonial civil servant, obsessed by bitter memories, breeding unhappiness and resentment, leading him to a futile act of treason. Now, in his dream, the narrator sees the way to freedom. The past may impose a burden of misery and causes for discontent, but the upstream swimmer can let the past, which weighs so heavily upon us, go.

It's a novel which invites quotation, for which I have no space here. There are passages on almost every page which call for reflection. But it is first of all a story — ah yes, the novel does tell a story, as Forster mournfully admitted, and thank God it does — and the story here is wonderfully moving. It's a novel which supports Ford Madox Ford's assertion that imaginative literature is more capable than any other art-form of making you think and feel at the same time.

I do not greatly admire Linklater's prewar novels. The 'high-spirited comedy and exuberant wit', for which he was praised then, now seem dated, too often forced. But his later novels when he was no longer in fashion are mostly good: notably *Position at Noon* (his own favourite among his books), which is certainly witty, but also restrained in its deployment of irony, *The House of Gair* (despite an outrageous use of coincidence) and *Roll of Honour*. Yet *The Dark of Summer* is the best, a novel of incomparable grace and strength, one which, like all great fiction, reveals something new at every reading. It's a novel I would love to have written, and I can never understand why it is so little known.

LIKELY LADS IN THEIR DAY
1 SEPTEMBER 2007

Simon Raven's first novel, *The Feathers of Death*, was published in 1959 when I was in my second year at Cambridge. We fell on it with glee, as I remarked, a few weeks after Raven's death, to a fellow-novelist, somewhat to her amazement. 'I've never read any of his books,' she said. 'I think my husband has.' Not so surprising perhaps. I doubt if he ever had many devoted female readers. What attracted us to the novel was not so much its for the time decidedly daring story — army officer's affair with blond, blue-eyed drummer Malcolm Harley — as the tone and style. This was nicely summed up by the *Sunday Times* reviewer, J. D. Scott, who found it difficult to believe that such an 'absurdly romantic, preposterously reactionary' novel should be so worthy of praise. But this of course was just what we loved about it. It appealed to our snobbishness, our champagne tastes. Moreover it was in its way very well-written and an agreeable change from the chippiness of the Irritable Young Men.

Another army novel had made a like impression a couple of years previously: James Kennaway's *Tunes of Glory*. In one sense this wasn't surprising. Most young writers of that generation had served in the forces. What was unusual about Raven and Kennaway was the warmth of their feeling for the army, a warmth which led them to romanticise it. In many ways the novels are very different. Kennaway's Eton and Sandhurst colonel is destroyed by the man he has supplanted, the former ranker Jock Sinclair who came into the regiment 'by way of Barlinnie Jail'. Yet both writers respond to the mystique of the army. Both novels end with a preposterously (to quote J. D. Scott) romantic funeral, and indeed, since the boy Harley's seducer Alastair Lynch is murdered by a private soldier bent on revenge, you might, stretching a point, say that both show us the crumbling of the old class-based army, something Raven at least deplored.

Kennaway and Raven had indeed a good deal in common. They were born within six or seven months of each other. Both went to public school — Raven Charterhouse, Kennaway Glenalmond. Both held national service commissions, but were just too young to serve in the war. Kennaway proceeded to Oxford, Raven to Cambridge. There was a certain glamour to both of them, raffish glamour in Raven's case. If we saw them as the literary heirs of Evelyn Waugh, it wasn't perhaps surprising, given that we ourselves were very young and ignorant of the world.

Neither, it may be said, fulfilled his promise. Kennaway died of a heart attack at the age of 40 while driving his Jaguar, probably too fast. He had published half a dozen novels, and though all are interesting and accomplished, none quite passes the test of staying fresh in the memory as *Tunes of Glory* does. Yet he was a serious, driven novelist as Raven never was, driven to the extent of manipulating his life and the lives of those around him in order to provide himself with material, in this somewhat resembling Scott Fitzgerald. 'It is becoming more and more ludicrous,' he wrote to his mother, 'to pretend that the point of my life is anything other than writing.'

Raven, though a thoroughly professional writer, who came to understand that 'to be an artist in any medium … requires moral determination and gruelling hard work', was quick to say that he wrote for money and to entertain educated readers of the upper and middle classes. At his best he was good. The first half-dozen novels in his *Alms for Oblivion* series remain worth reading. The first two especially are hard and sharp as he contrasts what he considered civilised values with money-hunger, materialism and the moral corruption that results from a lust for power. Kennaway incidentally does something similar in one of his best novels, *The Bells of Shoreditch*. Then Raven fell away. His novels , never less than readable, usually entertaining, topple into absurdity. I doubt if he cared. He had done his work, come through. Like, I would hope, many of my generation, I remain grateful to him; he gave us a lot of pleasure.

Tunes of Glory was made into a very good film starring Alec Guinness, with close-cropped red hair, as the ex-ranker colonel, and John Mills as the rival he destroys. Film rights of *The Feathers of Death* were sold, but I don't think the film was ever made. Too late now, I fear; impossible probably to make it without sending the book up. Yet there is a freshness to that novel which still has power to charm and a vein of genuine feeling that Raven rarely recaptured. He may not have lived up to our hopes for him — and much he would have cared about that! — but we weren't, I think, wrong to entertain them.

SOURCES OF INSPIRATION

15 SEPTEMBER 2007

The Craftsman is one of my favourite Kipling poems: 'Once, after long-drawn revel at The Mermaid, /He to the overbearing Boanerges /Jonson, uttered (if half of it were liquor, /Blessed be the vintage!)'

Then, in four stanzas he has Shakespeare reveal originals of his most famous female characters: Cleopatra, Juliet, Lady Macbeth, Ophelia, until: 'London wakened and he, imperturbable, /Passed from waking to hurry after shadows ... / Busied upon shows of no earthly importance?/ Yes, but he knew it!'

Kipling, master-craftsman himself, is concerned to show how little it may take to set a writer's imagination alight, how a mere hint may give birth to a character or scene or story. His Shakespeare found 'his very Cleopatra' in a Cotswold alehouse, 'Drunk with enormous, salvation-contemning/ Love for a tinker.' As for Juliet, he heard a gipsy girl 'Rail at the dawning', as he himself hid, 'Crouched in a ditch and drenched by the midnight/ Dews.' Lady Macbeth? Well, on Bankside, he saw a boy shrink from the task of drowning kittens, till his sister, aged seven, 'thrust 'em under, / Sombrely scornful.' And Ophelia? 'How on a Sabbath, hushed and compassionate — / She being known since her birth to the townsfolk — /Stratford dredged and delivered from Avon/ Dripping Ophelia.'

These are all of course conjectures, might-have-beens, one poet's imagination playing on the works of another. Kipling, compelling though I have always found his poem to be, doesn't suggest more than that. Nevertheless he is drawing attention to something important: the relation of art to life, the manner in which the artist draws from experience and then re-shapes it. This was something that fascinated him, as his account of the genesis of one of his finest and most puzzling stories shows:

> All I carried away from the magic town of Auckland was the face and voice of a woman who sold me beer at a little hotel there. They stayed at the back of my mind till ten years later when, in a local train of the Cape Town suburbs, I heard a petty officer from Simons Town telling a companion about a woman in New Zealand who 'never scrupled to help a lame dog or put her foot on a scorpion'. Then — precisely as the removal of a key-log in a timber-jam starts the whole pile — these words gave me the key to the face and voice at Auckland, and a tale called *Mrs Bathurst* slid into my mind, smoothly and orderly as floating timber on a bank-high river.

I find this utterly convincing, just as I can believe that Lady Macbeth's terrible line 'Give me the daggers' was born of the memory of a seven-year-old girl setting her face hard as she took over from a timid brother the grim task of drowning kittens. An image or phrase lodged in the memory may surface years later and serve as the key which will open a locked door. It's an unconscious act, and indeed the writer may not even identify the association as certainly as Kipling did in the case of *Mrs Bathurst*. This is why a novelist may sometimes be surprised by the resemblance to someone he knows taken by one of his characters. The assumption that characters in fiction have real-life models is often of course well-founded, but not always. So, for instance, it's generally agreed that Mr Dorrit in *Little Dorrit* is a portrait of Dickens's father. This may be so, but I shouldn't be surprised to learn that Dickens had no such conscious intention, that he may even have written quite a lot of the novel before the resemblance struck him.

Kipling wrote of the 'daemon' that on occasion took control of his pen. Stevenson said something similar. They meant that there were times when they wrote as if mind was absent from their work, the unconscious had taken over. Hemingway had the same idea; hence his insistence that he never thought about the book he was working on from when he finished his day's writing to the time he returned to his desk the following morning. That way, he said, your subconscious keeps working on it. The time for conscious thought comes later when you revise and, if you are Kipling, cut and cut and cut.

Probably most writers have this experience from time to time. Poets find lines come unbidden to their heads. Novelists are surprised by what their characters say or do. A flash of illuminating unsought memory sets a scene in motion. Something that critics will remark as a significant symbol appears of its own accord on the page. It's wonderful when this happens. There's only one caveat. It happens as often to bad writers as to good. Indeed some of the most utter tosh may have been written in an inspired trance.

THE MAGNUM OPUS OF COMPTION MACKENZIE

29 SEPTEMBER 2007

'You get no sense from him,' F. Scott Fitzgerald wrote after meeting Compton Mackenzie on Capri, 'that he feels his work has gone to pieces. He's not pompous about his present output. I think he's just tired. The war wrecked him as it did Wells and many of that generation.' Fitzgerald himself survives, on the strength of two and a half novels and perhaps a dozen short stories, but, except in Scotland, Mackenzie is, I surmise, more or less forgotten, and even in Scotland it's only *Whisky Galore* and his Highland farces which keep his name alive. It will surprise many to learn that Fitzgerald once idolised him, but *This Side of Paradise*, his first novel, is very much son of Mackenzie's *Sinister Street*.

The 1914-18 war, in which he worked as an intelligence officer in Greece, may indeed have left Mackenzie tired, but it hardly 'wrecked him'. Indeed, within a couple of years of Fitzgerald's dismissive judgment, he would publish *Vestal Fire*, the first of two Capri extravaganzas. The other is *Extraordinary Women*, scandalous at the time on account of its lesbian theme. Both books remain amusing and readable. If not as good as Norman Douglas's *South Wind*, they survive better than Aldous Huxley's comparable novels of conversation. Mackenzie was 13 years older than Fitzgerald, but outlived him by 32, writing to the end. Not bad going for someone 'wrecked' half a century earlier.

He made his reputation as an English Edwardian novelist; too much gush in his first books. *Sinister Street* was banned by libraries and highly praised by Henry James. This irritated Hugh Walpole, who saw himself as James's pet young novelist and was jealous of Mackenzie. 'Mackenzie, in spite of his cleverness, is no good,' he wrote, indignantly. 'Anyone who prefers Sinister Street to Sons and Lovers!' Well, I do. *Sinister Street* — splendid title — has its longueurs, but ranks with Maugham's *Of Human Bondage* as the best of the quasi-autobiographical English novels of the period. Ford Madox Ford thought it 'possibly a work of real genius'.

Much of his immediate post-war fiction is garrulous and dated, but in the Thirties he embarked on what was to be his major work, a huge rambling novel of his life and times, *The Four Winds of Love*. Eric Linklater, to whom one of the Winds was dedicated, thought he was only one of half-a-dozen people to have read the whole thing, and, if people are choked off before the end, it's not surprising, for the *North Wind*, treating principally of the hero John Ogilvie's commitment to Scottish nationalism, has long passages of boredom and is now very dated. Ogilvie himself, endlessly loquacious and pedagogic, a vehicle for Mackenzie's opinions about almost everything, is often thoroughly tiresome, partly because he is allowed to get the best of almost every argument. Nevertheless Edmund Wilson, himself an opinionated if not always acute critic, thought well of the book. 'There's something there,' he wrote, adding that the failure of British critics to give Mackenzie his due was evidence of 'London provincialism'. Wilson, like his friend Fitzgerald, had been a devotee of *Sinister Street*:

> The 'motif of utter foulness' is one of the most uncanny things in the book. You feel you are not walking on solid ground, but that it may give way at any moment, and let you into the sewer.

If the Winds sequence tails off, the first two parts, East and South, remain very good, stimulating, enjoyable, witty, occasionally moving. They feature the most interesting character he ever created. Emil Stern is a 16-year-old 'Jewish beauty' and intellectual when we first meet him in love with Ogilvie at St Paul's (St James's in the novel). Emil will become a fervent Marxist, a British consul in the Levant and successful espionage agent in the war. Later he will suppress his homosexuality by an act of will, marry a humourless Swedish woman, and go to prison in the Twenties for attempting to incite mutiny in His Majesty's Forces. (Mackenzie himself would be charged under the Official Secrets Act and tried at the Old Bailey after the publication of his own war memoirs.)

'The plot of the *Four Winds*,' his admirable biographer Andro Linklater wrote succinctly, 'is the twentieth century. It is the current of public affairs that carries the story forward, and the central characters reveal themselves through their discussion of these events.' To some extent the nature and ambition of the project account for Edmund Wilson's approval; he was a man of ideas himself, and a harsh judgment might be that he praised it for what it set out to be rather than for what it actually was.

It was almost the end of Mackenzie's serious novel-writing, but there was to be one late flowering: *Thin Ice*, published in 1956 when he was 73. I hope to write about it another time.

HOW SACRED IS SHAKESPEARE?

13 OCTOBER 2007

A couple of weeks ago I was at the Wigtown Book festival where I had been invited to give the first Magnus Magnusson Memorial Lecture. Magnus had been a great supporter of this festival — and no wonder, for it is quite charming — ever since it began when Wigtown was chosen as Scotland's official book town. That selection was a surprise, partly because this small Galloway town on the Solway Firth is ill-served by public transport. ('What's the quickest way to get to Wigtown from Edinburgh by public transport?' Answer: 'Fly to Belfast and take the ferry.'). Nevertheless it has been a great success, and the little town seems more prosperous on every visit. This year's festival attracted, among many others, Neal Ascherson, Louis de Bernières, John Walsh, Maggie Fergusson, R. F. Foster and *The Spectator*'s own James Delingpole.

The subject of my lecture was *Our Changing Language* and one of the questions put to me was this: 'Given the development of our language over the centuries, is Shakespearean English still generally comprehensible? Is there a case for rendering the plays into modern English?'

One's immediate reaction is, 'Of course not; the suggestion is heretical.' Moreover, given the fact that Shakespeare still holds the stage, there would appear to be absolutely no need for any modernisation of the text. Yet some have thought otherwise. A. L. Rowse, whose opinion of his own mastery of Tudor and Jacobean history and Shakespeare scholarship was not notably humble, did in fact produce modernised texts of some of the plays, though I doubt if his versions have ever been staged. Certainly the further we get from Shakespeare, the more difficult his language will seem. Half a century ago the Oxford scholar, Neville Coghill, produced a version of Chaucer's *Canterbury Tales* in contemporary English. It was published by Penguin and sold widely; generations of 'A' Level students have been grateful. Likewise churches now use the New English Bible rather than the Authorised Version, and Cranmer's *Book of Common Prayer* has been modernised.

If the suggestion that Shakespeare be updated seems an example of cultural vandalism, it's because, for many of us, the chief glory of Shakespeare is indeed the language, and it is his use of words which gives the keenest pleasure. Fair enough, but the worldwide appreciation of Shakespeare quite evidently doesn't depend on language. The plays are performed all over the world in I don't know how many different tongues. If French translations always seem rather flat to me, nevertheless his plays have held the stage in France ever since the early nineteenth century. One of the most gripping productions of any Shakespeare play I have ever seen was the Rustaveli company's *Richard III* — even though I didn't understand a word of the Georgian language in which it was given.

Puritanically-minded critics such as F. R. Leavis and L. C. Knights used to insist that the plays should be read as 'dramatic poems' and that it was vulgar or middlebrow to discuss the characters, in the fashion of A. C. Bradley, as if they were real people. Knights wrote a once famous essay, *How Many Children Had Lady Macbeth?*, deriding Bradley's approach to the plays.

Acute though much of their criticism was, it never seemed very convincing. After all, if the plays were primarily dramatic poems, it was strange that they should have been written for the stage, strange that actors should work so hard to get a sense of the characters they were playing, and strangest of all that these 'dramatic poems' should be performed successfully in other languages in theatres across the world. In short, it's evident that there is much more to the plays than the language, that they remain compelling on account of the dramatic situations and the fascination of the characters Shakespeare devised.

Happily, as I replied to my questioner, the day hasn't yet arrived when Shakespearean language is incomprehensible to theatre audiences here, even if one must admit that much will not be understood at first hearing and a good deal of the prose repartee in the comedies — and comic interludes in the tragedies — puzzling enough on the printed page, must baffle any audience not composed of Shakespearean scholars. Nevertheless our language is indeed changing so fast, and becoming so far removed from sixteenth-century English, that it is quite likely that future generations will find more and more in the plays obscure, even beyond their understanding. If this comes about, then there will indeed be demands for updated versions to enable audiences to appreciate the plays as dramatic works. It will be a loss, but the loss would be greater if the plays were never staged simply because the language had become incomprehensible. Perhaps A. L. Rowse was ahead of the game.

SYMPATHY FOR
THE OLD DEVIL
27 OCTOBER 2007

In his criticism of Sainte-Beuve's biographical method, Proust observes that it 'ignores what a very slight degree of self-acquaintance teaches us: that a book is a product of a very different self from the self we manifest in our habits, in our social life, in our vices.' I would not enter the argument stirred up by Professor Terry Eagleton's attack on Kingsley Amis if it weren't for the fact that those who have leapt — gallantly in the case of his second wife, Elizabeth Jane Howard — to Kingsley's defence have spoken of the man, rather than the writer. This is understandable. Nobody can be happy to have someone they have liked, and indeed loved, dismissed as 'a racist, anti-Semitic boor, a drink-sodden, self-hating reviler of women, gays and liberals'.

To do justice to Eagleton evidence to support his opinion may be found in Amis's letters. But letters are an imperfect guide. Few of us would care to be judged on throwaway lines written in letters to amuse friends. What, however, of the novels where what Proust calls 'the innermost self' (*le moi profond*) is revealed? I have the horrid suspicion that Professor Eagleton has either not read them or read them with inadequate attention.

Take drink. There's certainly a lot of drink and drunkenness in Amis's novels, and in the early ones — *Lucky Jim*, for instance — this is associated with having a good time and is matter for comedy. Later, *The Old Devils*, which won him the Booker Prize, is indeed 'drink-sodden', but there's not much suggestion of authorial approval. For the characters it's mostly a way of getting through

106

dreary, otherwise miserable, days. And in *The Folks that Live on the Hill* the horrors of alcoholism are made wretchedly clear.

Racist? Consider this exchange from *I Want It Now*. The setting is the American South. A boor — a genuine boor, Professor Eagleton — announces that blacks are inferior, 'and we in the South have the honest-to-God common sense to realise it ... The only way to keep the Negro in his place is by fear. The only argument he understands is the lash.'

'What you are saying is balls,' says Ronnie Appleyard, who has just become aware of a 'pure, authentic, violent sentiment of a liberal or progressive tendency'. 'And also extremely offensive, barbaric, inhumane, foolish, ignorant, out-moded and in the circumstances unforgivably rude.'

Now, while one should always be careful about ascribing a character's opinion to the author, I've no doubt that the reader is expected to agree with Ronnie rather than with the sentiments of the deep unreconstructed South.

Anti-gay? The few homosexual characters in the novels are almost always treated with sympathy and understanding. Examples: Hunter in *The Anti-Death League*, Bernard and Shorty in *Ending Up*, Jeremy in *You Can't Do Both*. In *The Old Devils* Charlie's gay brother is a morally admirable person who comes closer than anyone to making the egregiously selfish Alun Weaver feel ashamed of his behaviour. Homophobic sentiments tend to be expressed by characters whom we are invited to laugh at or disapprove of.

'A reviler of women'? A recurrent theme is certainly male inability to understand women and one novel, Stanley and the Women, may on one reading be described as misogynist. To the extent that it is so, this reflects Stanley's views and experience. On the other hand, puzzled and often irritated as Amis may have been by women's behaviour and expectations, all his heroes not only want women, but need them. Time and again, women are shown as behaving better than men, certainly as having higher moral standards. Jenny in *Take a Girl Like You* and *Difficulties with Girls* is not only attractive but an indisputably good person. With the possible exception of Rhiannon in *The Old Devils* she is quite the nicest character in the whole body of Amis's fiction. Rhiannon, modelled perhaps on Amis's first wife, Hillary, is warm, sympathetic, generous. She always behaves well and couldn't have been created by anyone who hated or reviled women.

There are certainly frightful, ghastly women in Kingsley's novels, but there are frightful, ghastly men too. A recurrent question throughout his fiction, right up to his last major novel, *You Can't Do Both*, is this: the will drives a man to behave like a shit —what is there to restrain him from being a complete shit?

Novels are written to explore questions rather than to answer them, and this one is well worth exploring. Robin, the philandering Amis-figure of that novel, gets his comeuppance from his admirable wife, Nancy. Reviewing it in 1994, I wrote:

> In his youth Amis might have been more on Robin's side than he is now, but perhaps not; he was always a moralist, though now one who seems more saddened than amused by the perversity of the human condition.

A moralist, yes, and one whose general tendency is, whatever Professor Eagleton may think, liberal.

MURDER MOST SERIOUS

10 NOVEMBER 2007

Raymond Chandler praised Dashiell Hammett for having given murder back to the sort of people who commit it. Given that he himself followed in Hammett's footsteps, this was an understandable remark, aimed at what might already have been called the classic English detective novel. 'Can't read Christie,' he told someone who had sent him a questionnaire. This wasn't quite true. In one letter he analyses, intelligently and judiciously, Christie's *Ten Little Niggers*; elsewhere, in an essay, *Casual Notes on the Mystery Novel*, he wrote that he was 'quite unmoved to indignation by The Murder of Roger Ackroyd's violation of the rule that "the suppression of facts by the narrator . . . is a flagrant dishonesty" because the dishonesty is rather cleverly arranged,' and in any case 'the whole arrangement of the story and of its *dramatis personae* makes it clear that the narrator is the only possible murderer.' He was also lavish in his praise of Michael Innes, most artificial of mystery writers. Nevertheless what he said about Hammett does reflect an impatience with the poison-in-the-fishpaste-sandwiches sort of crime novel that Agatha Christie wrote, and his conviction that the hard-boiled crime novel was more true to life and experience.

Judging by the sort of crime fiction now written, Chandler seems to have won the argument. With only a few exceptions — Simon Brett and Andrew Taylor in his Lydmouth novels, for instance — the crime novel in Britain as in the US generally owes more to Hammett and Chandler than to Christie. 'Murder is given back to the sort of people who commit it' and the amateur detective has given way to the policeman. Even when he is a rebel and loner, like Ian Rankin's Rebus, who may be held to owe more to Chandler's Marlowe or even Hammett's Sam Spade than to your average DI, he still can't altogether escape the requirements of police procedure, and this gives the fiction a realistic feel.

Yet Chandler's suggestion that only certain types of people commit murder is surely nonsense. Simenon knew better. Time and again, and not only in the Maigret novels, he shows us men and women brought by force of circumstances, obsession (his great subject), and even tricks of fate to the point of killing, and, unlike both Chandler and Hammett, he never downplays the seriousness of the crime. He knows that to commit murder is to cross a bridge, carrying you away from the common run of humanity.

In the hard-boiled crime novel murder becomes almost incidental, its horror diminished so to the point where it scarcely seems to matter. Many will know the story of how when *The Big Sleep* was being filmed, a telegram was sent to Chandler asking him who killed the chauffeur. The anecdote has it that he couldn't remember. '*Se non è vero, è ben trovato*,' for in this kind of novel, the crime itself often appears insignificant, murder merely a device to keep the plot moving. In Hammett's *Red Harvest* there are so many corpses that it's impossible to care about any of them. So the 'realistic' crime novel is in its own way as artificial as the classic English detective story, for in real life murder is rarely insignificant. It is disturbing, painful, alarming. It leaves people bereaved, miserable and at a loss. It remains a truly shocking act.

Artificial and contrived as her plots may be, Agatha Christie knew this. Hercule Poirot may be an absurd figure, Jane Marple an improbable investigator, but neither forgets, or allows the reader to forget, the enormity of murder. The novel may be framed as a challenge to the reader, even as a sort of game, but at some point Poirot will remind us that murder is the unforgivable crime, or

Miss Marple will declare that murder is evil and the murderer a very wicked man or woman.

There are admittedly exceptions to this generalisation. Nobody can take, for example, *Murder on the Orient Express* seriously, or regard Poirot's elucidation of the mystery as anything other than the agreeable conclusion to a clever parlour-game. Again, though the horror of murder is not glossed over in *The ABC Murders*, the premise of the book which has the killer committing two earlier, apparently unmotivated murders, to set the investigators of the killing that matters to him on a false trail, is absurd. So too is the murderer's unscrupulous use of a decoy.

Yet there is a sense in which Christie, at her best anyway, is more serious than Chandler and Hammett, simply because murder horrifies and disgusts her (even while she employs it for our amusement) as it doesn't apparently horrify them. It's like — if the comparison doesn't appear too far-fetched — the difference between *Macbeth* and a play like Kyd's *The Spanish Tragedy*. The murder of Duncan takes Macbeth across that bridge separating him from the common run of humanity; in Kyd's blood-stained play, as in the hard-boiled crime novel, murder is there to thrill, no more than that, its seriousness diminished, even obliterated.

NORMAN AT THE RITZ

24 NOVEMBER 2007

Andrew O'Hagan wrote a very nice piece about Norman Mailer in the *Daily Telegraph* last week. Affectionate and admiring, it was just the sort of tribute a young writer should pay to a senior one, and it was pleasant to learn how encouraging Mailer had been to O'Hagan and indeed to other young writers. This is as it should be — a handing on of the torch. No doubt this was easier for Mailer than for less successful elderly writers who find themselves elbowed out of the way by younger generations, and quite possibly dropped by their publishers. Nevertheless it's commendable, jealousy or envy being sins to which writers are prone.

I only once saw Mailer. That was more than 40 years ago, in the downstairs bar of the Ritz presided over by the incomparable Laurie Ross, famous for his Gin Rickeys and Dry Martinis. It was then my favourite place in London. Laurie was an exceptionally nice man who made all his customers feel welcome and important. He would also cash you a cheque, admittedly only for £5 on top of your bar bill, but a fiver went a long way in the 1960s, even in the West End of London — a night in the Savoy Turkish Baths in Jermyn Street cost less than a pound then.

Mailer was sitting alone in a corner of the bar looking, surprisingly, like a little boy lost. Probably he was only tired. I was tempted to approach him, then realised I couldn't honestly pretend to being a fan, for I had become bored with *The Naked and the Dead* halfway through and hadn't got even that far with

Barbary Shore. Even so, I might well, after another Gin Rickey, have plucked up the courage to speak to him, for I was young enough to be thrilled by the chance to meet a famous writer. Then he was joined by Cyril Connolly and the opportunity slipped away. A couple of years later I bought a collection of Mailer's journalism, *Cannibals and Christians*, with its dedication 'To Lyndon Johnson, whose name inspired young men to cheer for me in public', and regretted my failure to accost him, for the journalism, though often crazy, had a wonderful vitality and was more exciting and satisfying than the novels I had failed to finish. I don't know how it reads now. Perhaps I would rather not know. But it mattered to me then.

It may be he was always a better journalist and essayist, speaking in his own unmistakable voice. Yet the novel, which he called 'the Great Bitch in our life', was something that, as he put it, he could 'never be rid of', and if his most ambitious work of fiction, *Ancient Evenings*, seemed to me impenetrable, a real turkey, one couldn't deny the gallantry of his attempt.

I suspect that Mailer was a victim of his early success which made him a celebrity. Celebrity of the sort he enjoyed is not good for a novelist. It puts him at the centre of things. He is no longer the onlooker, the figure in the corner taking notes. Hemingway suffered the same fate, but Mailer had resources denied to him. For me, the best of his books is the one about Lee Harvey Oswald. It's a disturbing book in many ways, but the principal one is this: the society in which Oswald moved in his years in the Soviet Union seemed so much more intelligent, serious and civilised than the America where he grew up and to which he returned. This was not perhaps a fair comparison. In the US he mixed with what Americans disagreeably call 'trailer trash'; in the USSR he lived among people who read Tolstoy and Chekhov and went to concerts of classical music; he didn't meet the derelicts and social failures. Nevertheless, the contrast was indeed disturbing and thought-provoking. Mailer knew this and wrote a book which was as honest as it was enthralling. There's another reason why this book was more satisfying than the novels. He was telling a story which he hadn't had to invent, and invention was never his strongest suit.

Yet to the end he believed, as O'Hagan wrote, in the value of the novel, the importance of imaginative literature. At the same time he knew that 'a writer, no matter how great, is never altogether great; a small part of him remains a liar'. And that is a truth that all of us who write novels and aim to make them as good as it is possible for us to make them, must, shamefacedly, acknowledge. We cheat to conceal out weaknesses. Mailer, for all his faults, was more honest than most in his readiness to admit this, and I regret that I didn't have the nerve to approach him that evening in the Ritz, even if he might have given me the brush-off.

THE ENDURING MYSTERY OF
MRS BATHURST

8 DECEMBER 2007

'Listen, Bill,' wrote P. G. Wodehouse (in a letter published in *Performing Flea*), 'something really must be done about Kip's *Mrs Bathurst*. I read it years ago and didn't understand a word of it. I thought to myself, "Ah, youthful ignorance!" A week ago I re-read it. Result: precisely the same.'

Wodehouse is not alone in finding the story baffling. At once rambling and compressed, told entirely in reminiscent and speculative conversation, it is powerful but murky. You may feel it is a masterpiece yet be unable to determine just what happens. Summarising it is difficult, but, for the benefit of anyone who doesn't know the story, here goes.

Four men meet on a beach in South Africa and talk as they drink beer: an unnamed narrator (Kipling himself?), Inspector Hooper of the Cape Government Railways who has just come down from up-country, Pyecroft of the Royal Navy, an old acquaintance of the narrator, and Sergeant Pritchard of the Royal Marines. They speak first about old shipmates and an experience in Vancouver for which Pyecroft was court-martialled. Then the talk turns to one Vickery, known as 'Click', on account of his ill-fitting false teeth, a detail that arouses Hooper's curiosity. Vickery, it seems, had deserted ship and never been seen or heard of again.

'Who was she?' the narrator asks. 'She kep' a little hotel at Hauraki — near Auckland', is the reply. This is Mrs Bathurst, a widow, who 'never scrupled to feed a lame duck or set 'er foot on a scorpion at any time of 'er life.' Mrs Bathurst, with her 'blindish way o' looking', has 'It' . (First use of the expression?) Vickery, a married man with a 15-year-old daughter, becomes obsessed with her, on the strength of a couple of meetings.

Cut back to South Africa. Vickery takes Pyecroft to the cinema. (The story is set at a time when moving pictures were an astonishing novelty.) There is a film of the Western Mail coming into Paddington, and then 'slowly, from be'ind two porters — carryin' a little reticule an' looking from side to side — comes out Mrs Bathurst. There was no' mistakin' that walk.' Night after night Vickery compels Pyecroft to watch the snatch of film before taking him on a tour of the bars. The show moves on up-country. Vickery deserts — to see her again. Before he does so, he tells Pyecroft to remember that he is not a murderer because his 'lawful wife' died in childbirth six weeks after he set sail.

Now Hooper tells of how he came on two corpses up-country, struck by lightning, reduced to charcoal. One had false teeth. 'Permanent things false teeth are,' he says. 'You read about 'em in all the murder trials.'

Vickery is dead, no question about that. ('Thank Gawd', says Pyecroft, remembering his face on their cinema- and bar-evenings.) But whose is the other body? Nicolas Freeling, in an essay in his fascinating book, *Criminal Convictions*, has no doubt that it is Mrs Bathurst herself, and that Vickery, in his despairing obsession, has deliberately attracted the lightning. 'It is inconceivable,' Freeling writes, 'to drag in a new figure, previously unheard of, on the last page. The story is called *Mrs Bathurst* and she is the major character throughout, the more vividly so for being scarcely seen.'

This is good sense. Nevertheless, difficulties remain. If the other corpse is indeed hers, how and when did she come to Africa? Had Vickery arranged to meet her there, or did he happen on her by chance? If their meeting was arranged, and if he indeed 'deliberately attracted the lightning', why? What has she refused him?

She was last seen in the film-clip alighting from the train at Paddington, and looking around as if she was expecting someone to meet her. Who? Vickery himself?

And that remark about his 'lawful wife': was he hinting that he had contracted a bigamous marriage with Mrs Bathurst? Harry Ricketts, in his biography of Kipling, calls the 'cinematograph the device through which Vickery saw his lover on screen and was convinced he was being haunted.' If that's correct, and he met Mrs Bathurst by chance 'up-country' — but, again, how did she get there? — and he thought her a ghost — the ghost of the woman he had already killed, in England perhaps — that might explain why he attracted the lightning, if indeed he did.

Wodehouse was right to be puzzled. I'm puzzled myself, despite having read the story at least a dozen times. Yet I'm sure it's a masterpiece, and I would hazard that its true theme is the ultimate impossibility of fully knowing another human being. That sounds banal; but it's not when dramatically, if obscurely, expressed as it is here.

There are mysteries beyond explanation.

WOULD THEY HAVE ENDED UP GRUMPY OLD MEN?

12 JANUARY 2008

The transition from iconoclastic youth to crusty age is common enough. The emergence of Martin Amis as a critic of Islam (at least in some of its manifestations) may be an expression of solidarity with his old friends Salman Rushdie and Christopher Hitchens, or it may be that, as Terry Eagleton suggests, he is turning into his father. Certainly Kingsley may be held to have gone that way, and many of us, as the years pass, do indeed find ourselves resembling Dad. This must be a disturbing thought, often, for our sons. Those whom the gods love die young — before that happens. 'When Mozart was my age,' as Tom Lehrer used to say, 'he'd been dead for years'. 'Lucky man' is the unspoken thought.

The triumvirate of Romantic poets achieved only 92 years between them, Byron dying at 36, Shelley at 30 and Keats at a mere 26. Byron admittedly felt old before his time: 'If thou regret'st thy youth, why live?/ The land of honourable death/ Is here: up to the Field, and give/ Away thy breath.' The disillusion of this, his last poem, was doubtless in part a matter of convention, but if he felt exhausted, it was no wonder. He had packed more into the 18 years of adult life than most of us manage in 50. Nevertheless it's tempting to speculate how each would have developed if he had lived as long as Wordsworth or Tennyson. Shelley and Byron might well have done so, their deaths being fortuitous: drowning in Shelley's case, a fever contracted in the unhealthy lagoon of Missolonghi in Byron's. It's improbable that Keats could have survived tuberculosis, but suppose he had, or had never contracted the disease, would he have continued to pour out poetry — perhaps eventually finding himself observing, mournfully, like Tennyson, that he could do anything and everything with the English language but had nothing, or nothing left, to say? I prefer to think that with his intelligence, his curiosity about other people and sympathy with them, his lively sense of humour, he might have turned to writing novels; and, if he had done so, the marvellous vivacity of his letters suggests that they would have been wonderful. 'The unwritten novels of John Keats'; fine chapter for a counter-factual History of English Literature.

What of Shelley? Would he have remained a Man of the Left, being scooped-up, white hair streaming, by police as he took part in a sit-down demonstration in Trafalgar Square? Or would he as Sir Percy Shelley, Bart, have put all that behind him, becoming a pillar of the Establishment? Would the author of the tract *The Necessity of Atheism* have ended up as a churchwarden? Bertrand Russell or T. S. Eliot? He might have gone either way, for he was the perfect type of the intellectual always attracted to extreme positions. So would Shelley in his seventies have found himself lining up with Carlyle, Ruskin, Tennyson and Charles Kingsley in defence of Governor Eyre who had displayed what John Stuart Mill called 'brutal recklessness' in suppressing a Black rebellion in Jamaica? I suspect he might.

And Byron? Ah Byron! Harold Nicolson once wrote an essay entitled *If Byron had become King of Greece* (published in a 1930s collection of ventures into counter-factual history), but, sadly, I recall no more than the title. It's more likely, I think, that, his reputation restored by his exploits in Greece, he would have returned to England to resume his seat in the House of Lords. Would he have been eager for Parliamentary Reform, even a minister in Grey's Whig Government alongside his friend John Cam Hobhouse? It's certainly conceivable. But Byron could never — surely? — have sat easily to Party, and there was always a Tory reactionary streak in him —

witness his early sympathy for the Luddite machine-breakers. He would have had little sympathy with the new Industrial Age, and his Liberalism, though sincere, stopped well short of any approval of democracy. It's not difficult to imagine him as an aloof, scornful and misanthropic reactionary, detesting the vulgar commercialism of the Railway Age and subsiding into a disgruntled disaffection with his times, not unlike Evelyn Waugh's or indeed Kingsley Amis's, sharing Matthew Arnold's distaste for 'this strange disease of modern life,/ With its sick hurry, its divided aims, / Its heads overtax'd, its palsied hearts.' One pictures him, all too easily, as a bored and fretful 'grand seigneur'. Walter Scott once suggested to him that he would end in the Roman Catholic Church, and that too seems a probable and, in his case, melancholy, destination.

But he was spared that. They were all spared the pains and disgruntlement of advancing years, and so they remain, like the figures on the Grecian Urn, 'For ever warm and still to be enjoy'd,/ For ever panting and for ever young.'

SCRIBBLE, SCRIBBLE, SCRIBBLE

22 MARCH 2008

Why do we write? Dr Johnson had no doubts, or pretended to have none: 'no man but a blockhead ever wrote, except for money'. This is manifestly false, unless you make writing for some other reason one of your definitions of the word 'blockhead'. In any case it's not true of Johnson himself. Despite the indolence for which he reproached himself, he was an assiduous correspondent, writing long, thoughtful letters to his friends. Likewise, there are those who — obsessively — keep journals or diaries without, until recently anyway, expecting ever to profit from them.

The American novelist Jay McInerney has suggested that writing comes 'out of a deep well of loneliness and a desire to fill some gap. No one in his right mind would sit down to write a book if he were a well-adjusted, happy man.' This too is not quite nonsense, but comes close to being so. What about P. G. Wodehouse, by all accounts as happy as a lark, who was able to say 'I love writing', even though he also said that his way of working was to 'put a sheet of paper in the typewriter and curse a bit'.

There are writers of course who seem always to have worn a hair shirt, Conrad for instance who claimed that the sight of a pen and inkwell made him angry. His letters are full of moans about the difficulty of writing; it's a dismal trade that is making him ill. Nevertheless it was the trade he chose and he stuck at it. Surely there was some satisfaction to be found.

It may be that many of us do indeed take to writing because we are not, as Beryl Bainbridge has said, very good at living. So we try to make sense of things on paper instead. This may be why success is so often bad for a writer; it allows him to suppose he has mastered life. Complacency sets in; he is less curious about himself and other people, and his work suffers.

There are simpler explanations. Ambition is one — the desire to be well thought of. Being a writer may not get you a better table at a restaurant, but it does make you more interesting, to some people at least. Their initial interest may well be disappointed on further acquaintance, but while it exists, it is gratifying. Orwell, despite asserting that everything he wrote was in the cause of advancing democratic socialism, was honest enough to admit that the desire to be praised and make a show in the world was one motive for writing. For anyone who lacked confidence in youth or had a thin time of it at school, writing is a form of revenge. Even the most self-effacing of writers is crying out 'look at me' in every book or even newspaper article.

More admirable is the simple pleasure to be had from making something, common to the practice of any art or craft. To bring into being what did not previously exist, and to present it in an agreeable shape, is deeply satisfying — even if the final result is always inevitably less than you looked to achieve. Plato was right: the ideal work of art exists only in the imagination and the reality must always disappoint. Fortunately however, in the least satisfactory work, there will usually be some pages, some scenes, some characters that delight their creator, and so persuade him to go on. This is why Eric Linklater, a couple of years before his death, was able to say that the best times in his life had been when he was working on a novel and it was going well.

Scott Fitzgerald thought it was 'a hell of a profession' — I prefer the word trade; also that 'you don't write because you want to say something; you write because you have something to say'. That's questionable. If you have something to say, you write an article, not a novel. A novel is, for writer and reader alike, a voyage of exploration; in the writer's case it's a way of entering unknown territory and finding out what he thinks and feels. If he can take the reader with him all the way to the end, so much the better. But for him the journey itself is enough. Curiosity sets narrative going and the writer, like the reader, will, if all goes well, find himself surprised by much that he writes. Write because you have something to say? No: it's a novel, not a tract or argument. The old line — how do I know what I think till I see what I've said? — is more to the point.

Finally it's an addiction. Few novelists retire — and not only because they can't afford to. Without a book to work on, we wouldn't know how to get through the day.

To that extent, writing is an escape from boredom; also, oddly, from yourself.

ONLY A DEPRESSIVE?

31 MAY 2008

A fortnight ago Sam Leith, reviewing Neil Powell's book on the Amises, father and son, wrote:

> Powell is insistent — and for all I know dead right, but that's hardly the point — that Kingsley was a sufferer from depression. Of the last sentence of *The Anti-Death League* ('There isn't anywhere to be.'), he writes: 'This — the last sentence especially — is the authentic voice of depression, and only a depressive could have written it.' You may wonder where that untestable assertion gets us.

You may indeed, though the answer is pretty obvious: not very far. Powell has fallen into a trap that catches many critics and also, though perhaps less often, ordinary readers: the assumption that everything in a novel or play derives from the writer's experience, rather than his imagination. It's absurd.

Take another example: 'To-morrow, and to-morrow, and to-morrow,/ Creeps in this petty pace from day to day,/ To the last syllable of recorded time;/ And all our yesterdays have lighted fools/ The way to dusty death.' Here too we may say, with Powell, 'is the authentic voice of depression', at least as authentic as that heard in the line he quotes. But would you say that 'only a depressive could have written it'? Or would it be more sensible to conclude that Shakespeare has imagined how Macbeth should feel as this moment when he has just been told of his wife's death and when the props of his existence are shuddering? Shakespeare had no need to be himself on the point of despair; all he had to do was imagine Macbeth's feelings and find the right words for him to speak.

It's easy to demonstrate the idiocy of the sort of assertion Powell makes. Suppose you write a nasty and violent rape scene so well that it is utterly and horribly convincing. You might be rather pleased with it. But you would reasonably be offended if some critic came along to assure the world that 'only a rapist could have written it'.

Almost 20 years ago my friend, the poet Robert Nye, wrote a remarkable novel about Gilles de Rais, once a companion-in-arms of Joan of Arc, then brought to trial charged with witchcraft and heresy, sacrilege and the practice of unnatural crimes against children of both sexes, ending with their murder for his delight. He was convicted and executed at Nantes in 1440. Now I can think of no one less like Gilles de Rais than Robert Nye, also of nobody more capable of thoroughly imagining him. He could do so because, in the words of his narrator — a priest who served as Gilles' chaplain — he understands that 'Not madmen or monsters do these things. We do. The imagination of man is evil from his youth. The only hope for us is: some do not.' Reviewing the novel, I observed, 'This is as true in the age of Auschwitz as it was in the fifteenth century.'

None of this means of course that novelists and playwrights don't often draw on personal experience. Most of the best novels about addictions are written by addicts. Nevertheless experience only takes you a short distance. Fiction — plays and films as well as novels — is made from experience, observation and imagination; and the last is the most important of the three, for it is imagination which enables you to illuminate what you have lived through, and what you have seen or heard, and by playing on this double experience give it the significance which a bald recital lacks.

Experience provides material. Observation adds to it. This is important, for without material there is nothing to work on, and indeed many writers exhaust their material, and their work withers. But material without imagination is worth very little. Some of the greatest writers have, outwardly, led quiet lives without much incident; one thinks, for instance, of Henry James and Thomas Mann, both of whom indeed seem to have chosen self-denial rather than self-fulfilment. It is quite possible that Shakespeare too belonged to this category, and that self-denial fostered his extraordinary imagination, enabling him to inhabit the characters he created and find the words in which they reveal themselves. The source of a story may be the merest incident on which the imagination plays. The sight of a couple in a restaurant had V. S. Pritchett asking, 'what does he see in her?' and then employing his imagination in the search for an answer. The writer can imagine a man in despair, suffering acute depression, and then contentedly join his wife for tea and scones.

Incidentally I've just picked up *The Anti-Death League*, and the last sentence is not that quoted. It is in fact, 'The steering failed to respond': a road accident in which a dog is killed. Kingsley Amis, a non-driver, nevertheless managed to write this sentence. Which may prove something; my argument perhaps.

OBLIVION IS THE COMMON LOT

28 JUNE 2008

Callimachus (fl. fourth century BC), admired by Catullus, Ovid and Propertius, was the author of some 800 books, including a 120-volume catalogue of the Greek writers whose works were to be found in the famous library of Alexandria. Of his own work, only six hymns, 64 epigrams, the fragment of an epic, and a description of the method he employed to compile his catalogue, survive today. Harvey's Oxford Companion to Classical Literature also tells us that 'his is the proverbial saying, *"mega biblion, mega kakon"*', which means, if my rusty Greek has not seized up completely, 'big book, big bad', a sentiment to which reviewers, confronted by an 800-page biography, may often give wholehearted assent.

The fate of his works reminds us that oblivion is the lot of most books, and that authors who hope for literary immortality are usually disappointed. Publishers often used to employ the back pages of books to advertise their other publications, and few authors can read without a sinking heart the praise accorded to novels which are now quite forgotten and writers of whom they have never heard.

Samuel Johnson took a characteristically robust view:

No Place affords a more striking Conviction of the Vanity of human Hopes, than a publick Library ... Of the innumerable Authors whose Performances are thus treasured up in magnificent Obscurity, most are undoubtedly forgotten, because they have never deserved to be remembered, and owed the Honours which they once obtained, not to

Judgement or to Genius, to Labour or to Art, but to the Prejudice of
Faction, the Stratagems of Intrigue, or the Servility of Adulation.

'Ouch!' may be the response to this statement of a melancholy
truth, followed by the malicious listing of colleagues and rivals (for
all colleagues are also rivals) who owe their success today to just
such prejudice, stratagems and servility. Not that there is much
comfort in this.

Survival — setting aside the accidents of time which have seen
the greater part of the work of ancient authors like Callimachus
lost — depends doubtless on merit. Those authors whose works
are remembered and read are the few who do not deserve to be
forgotten. But how many, even among those who are remembered,
are still read, and, of those who are, how much of their output?
What of Johnson himself? Belloc thought that you should read
Rasselas once a year because there is so much well-expressed wisdom
there, but how few of us are likely to do so — how few may have
read it even once.

You remember the books you read and enjoyed and learned
from when you were young, and you wonder who reads them now.
Maybe nobody does. Maybe they linger only in the memory of a
'Happy Few', the number diminishing every year. Maybe it would
be a mistake to read some of them again: Nigel Dennis's *Cards of
Identity*, for instance. It was exhilarating to read it at 18. Now, apart
from the memory of the enjoyment I got from it, I recall only one
line: 'All trees are oaks to Presidents.' Or perhaps to headmasters
and housemasters, I thought then. Ten or so years later, there was
a brilliant little novel, a tale of corruption, called *Ask Agamemnon*.
The author's name was, I think, Hall. Did she? — yes, surely she —
write anything else? Other more famous novelists — Snow, Angus
Wilson, Elizabeth Bowen, Joyce Cary, William Sansom, L. P. Hartley,
William Cooper — seem to exist now only in a sort of shadowland;
but all in their different ways once gave me pleasure, mattered to me.

Living writers elbow dead ones out of the way, and will themselves be pushed aside in time. Brian Moore, another who has received that elbow in the ribs, has his novelist-hero of *An Answer from Limbo* say: '"Aschenbach's whole soul, from the very beginning, was bent on fame." That sentence from Thomas Mann now strikes me as false. Fame is not the prize; the prize is the doing of the thing itself.' No doubt, no doubt. Nevertheless, a little later: 'Kierkegaard and Camus, Dostoevsky and Gide — I spun the circular racks at the bus terminal paperback stand. Would there be room for me?', he asks. Good question, the sort of one we all put, though today's novelists may well wonder, enviously, at a bus terminal bookstand where books by Gide and Camus were to be found. Perhaps Callimachus is fortunate that as many as 64 of his epigrams survive. One of them at least does more than just survive in an English version: 'They told me, Heraclitus, they told me you were dead…' A pleasant voice, a nightingale, still awake, after almost two and a half thousand years. 'Strange Comfort Afforded by the Profession', as Malcolm Lowry put it.

SIMON GRAY: R.I.P.

23 AUGUST 2008

Ten, eleven weeks ago I had an email from Simon Gray to say that the tumour on his lung hadn't grown; so he was all right till his next scan in four months' time. Now he is dead and I wonder if they didn't tell him the truth then, or if the thing took a sudden spurt. The latter, surely; he wasn't someone to conceal bad news from. 'I am always eager to acknowledge the worst,' he wrote in the last published volume of his diaries, 'and often in advance of the evidence.'

A day or two later came another email. 'Now that I know I'm not going to die for four months I'll have to find something to write. Any ideas?' I replied that there was an episode in that last diary, about having to sack a talented young American actor from the cast of the New York revival of *Butley*, which might make a short play. 'Why don't you write it?' he said. Perhaps I'll try to, if only 'in memoriam'.

I hadn't seen him for years, nevertheless always thought of him as one of my real friends. There were many, some themselves now dead, like Alan Bates and Ian Hamilton, others like his beloved wife Victoria and Harold and Antonia Pinter, who were, obviously, very much closer to him. They shared his life, as I didn't. Yet our friendship, dating from Cambridge days, was kept alive by occasional letters, postcards, latterly emails. A couple of weeks ago I wrote here about Malcolm Lowry, of whom one of his friends said, 'even a sight of the old bastard cheers me up for days'. A note from Simon had the same effect on me.

130

SIMON GRAY: R.I.P.

He was a couple of years older, had spent time teaching, hilariously, in retrospect at least, at a French school before coming to Trinity, and at first I was a bit shy, even wary of him. He was bigger, burlier, sharp-witted and much more intelligent. The shyness soon abated and I delighted in his company. I picture him most clearly at the poker table, black lock of hair falling — not exactly like James Bond — over his left eye, smoke curling into the blue-grey air, a glass of whisky (Glenfarclas) by his side, as he successfully bluffed me and scooped the pool. He was the funniest man I knew, with such a vein of fantasy and laconic wit. 'I wonder,' he wrote recently, 'if we knew at Cambridge what good times we were having.' Perhaps we didn't, but they glow in memory.

His best plays will last, as long as there is an audience for intelligent theatre. His rambling, apparently artless, really artful, diaries, wholly original in tone and manner, delighted many who haven't been in a theatre in years.

Simon was a champion grumbler, no silver linings to his clouds. The ugliness and bad manners of contemporary England depressed him, though he made sport of his anger and disapproval. In one of these diaries he remarked that his mother had been a great slapper and cuffer of her sons, and would these days have been carted off to prison, 'but then,' he added, 'we live in exceptionally stupid times'. So indeed we do. 'State education,' he wrote to me recently, 'still controlled by the "*enfants sauvages*" of the Sixties. We should have strung them from lamp-posts while we had the chance.' Missed our opportunity, alas.

But he also wrote beautifully of those people and things that he loved, of family and friends, dogs and cats, books, poetry, movies, the theatre (love-hate there perhaps), Greece, Barbados, cricket. Illuminatingly too: I recall a passage in which he says that Andrew Flintoff made him think of a fine, upstanding yeoman chap in a

Housman poem, to whom something nasty will happen in the last verse.

He was very, typically, and, despite everything, proudly English, and, like so many typical Englishmen, half a Scot (grandparents from Greenock). I remarked on this once, observing that his eagerness to look on the black side was very Scottish, and, though he often muttered with gloomy disapproval of 'scottiness' he emailed me, 'You're quite right about my scotchness by the way — I suspect I'll soon grow an accent, as my father did at the age of 70'.

Well, sadly, we won't hear him speak in that accent, but his other nightingales are still awake. In his last diary he told of how he often went to sit by the grave of his much-loved younger brother Piers, dead at 50 or so of the alcoholism from which Simon escaped, and found comfort there. I should like some day to sit by his. 'What thou lovest well will not be reft from thee.' Having said that, I can't remember whether he cared for Ezra Pound, or classed him with Auden as a phoney.

IN DEFENCE OF THE DEMOTIC
6 SEPTEMBER 2008

'The result is a minor masterpiece, so good that one can even forgive the author's affected forays into demotic English ('don't' and 'wouldn't' for 'did not' and 'would not', etc).' Setting aside the writer's mistake — 'don't' being the contraction of 'do not' rather than 'did not' — this sentence brought me up sharp, all the more so because it was the conclusion of Jonathan Sumption's review in this magazine of John Guy's book about Thomas and Margaret More; and Jonathan Sumption is not only a *Spectator* reviewer, but also one of our finest historians.

'Affected forays into demotic English' is a splendid magisterial put-down. Poor Mr Guy! Poor me too, now I think of it, for I see that in my most recent column, delivered before I had read Mr Sumption's condemnation of 'demotic English' — that is, English as it is spoken – I was guilty of three such 'affected forays' in the first paragraph alone: one 'hadn't', one 'didn't' and one 'wasn't'. Should I blush with shame?

In my defence I might say that the style of this column is, generally, relaxed; that it doesn't aspire to the dignity of History, as I suppose Mr Guy's book does; that instead it is couched in conversational tones which may make the use of such contractions permissible. (And, indeed, I see that a 'doesn't' has already slipped, in unconsidered fashion, into this paragraph.)

Then I might seek allies among other contributors to *The Spectator*. In the same issue as Mr Sumption's review, I am happy to find Matthew Parris and Paul Johnson both making similar

133

'affected forays' into the demotic. Mr Parris indeed does so on ten occasions in his article, while our sub has put a 'don't' in its heading. As for Paul Johnson — surely an authority with whom few would argue? — he began the last paragraph of his essay with the observation: 'But we can't all be wise.' How very true!

Yet on reflection I feel more inclined to attack than defend. Is it perhaps Mr Sumption whose 'foray' may fairly be termed 'affected'? The contractions he objects to are not only common. They are normal in spoken English, and it is a rare and, one might say, decidedly affected person who doesn't employ them every day in conversation. This is not only usual but useful, for it allows one to make a distinction not otherwise available. 'That isn't so' isn't (is not?) quite the same as 'that is not so'.

Of course there is a difference between the written and the spoken language, things being permissible in the latter which one may reasonably object to in the former. Yet it is also the case that written English deteriorates the further it is removed from the way in which we speak. You have only to read the 'mission statement' from any public organisation to know this. The worst English is that in which you can no longer hear a voice.

Anyone who takes trouble over the way he writes should know the rules and conventions of the language, but should also be prepared to depart from them on occasion. Some of the so-called rules are arbitrary, even silly. Some are what Kingsley Amis called 'fancied prohibitions dear to ignorant snobs'. The example he gave was ending a sentence with a preposition. This is something we all do in speech and should be happy to do in writing. 'As Fowler famously observed,' he wrote, 'the power of saying … "People worth talking to" instead of "People with whom is it worth our while to talk" is not one to be lightly surrendered.' Quite so.

Written English is necessarily more structured than spoken English, which, as any tape recording will demonstrate, is often incoherent, rambling, full of hesitations and broken-backed sentences, but the careful writer will try to keep the sound of his voice in what he writes. The spoken language — the demotic — employs contractions all the time. Why should the writer shun them?

LOVING OR HATING
YOUR SUBJECT
20 SEPTEMBER 2008

'Reviewing two books about Hemingway in *The Spectator* (19 August 2006) Caroline Moorehead asked: 'How far is it right for biographers to write about subjects they so patently dislike? Hemingway is portrayed as bullying, narcissistic, foul-tempered, slovenly and miserly.' No doubt he was all these things, some of the time anyway, but the question remains a fair one. In his defence, the author of the book in which Hemingway is so portrayed, Stephen Koch, might argue that all these epithets might also be applied to the Hemingway depicted by his widow, Mary Welsh Hemingway, and by his admiring friend or, in some people's opinion, sidekick, A. E. Hotchner. The difference of course is that in their books we are also given the attractive, life-enhancing side of Hemingway's character. If Hotchner's Hemingway often seems boring and boorish, it's also clear that till near the end Hotchner loved the company of his hero; and there is tragic pathos in his detailed account of Hemingway's descent into depression and paranoia as he lurched, lost and bewildered, towards his suicide.

Doing a demolition job on the dead, especially the recently dead, may be profitable. It's also usually unattractive. One of Graham Greene's biographers, Michael Shelden, presented him, according to Piers Paul Read, as 'a selfish shit and bogus Catholic'. Many who knew Greene, as his biographer didn't, found the book repulsive. Shelden's Greene wasn't the man they had known. One might answer Caroline Moorehead's question by saying that if you want to write a hostile biography, pick a subject who is still

136

alive, and in a position to hit back. At least that takes rather more courage.

Things can be more complicated, however. The hostile biography isn't necessarily born in hostility. A good example is Roger Lewis's of Anthony Burgess. The young Lewis admired and was dazzled by Burgess. By the time Burgess was dead and Lewis came to write his biography, he

> had decided that his sense of separateness, initially heroic, has come to appear pathetic; what's so big about being unfit for ordinary life and too proud to deal with problems in the material world?... His success came from impressing people who didn't know better ...

— like indeed the young Roger Lewis who by the time he wrote the book found himself asking 'what lack or absence in me was being compensated for?' His Burgess is a man who promoted himself as a great writer, but never wrote a great book. *Earthly Powers* is 'a pastiche of a great novel'. He is 'essentially bogus'. Everything in his public performances is 'directed towards projecting a genial persona, but clearly he wasn't genuinely genial. He knew you weren't his equal, and I find this an insult.' (Not the impression I had in my few conversations with Burgess, but perhaps he fooled me, as Lewis believes he fooled him for years.) One could go on quoting. Lewis's book is full of good things, of pithy judgments, many of them astute. It's certainly a demolition job, if a high-class one. The image of the great writer which Burgess worked so hard to construct is shattered.

It's in many ways an unfair book and there are times when it seems that Lewis did eventually 'patently dislike' his subject. Perhaps for this reason it shouldn't have been written. Yet it's not wholly unsympathetic, because Lewis himself as well as Burgess is the subject, and it's a record of his disillusionment, bitterness arising from a love and hero-worship that have gone wrong. It may not be fair, but who ever writes fairly from such a perspective?

The best biographies are sympathetic. Their authors don't gloss over their subjects' failures and faults of character, but they don't seek to do them down. The biographer who sets out to mock his subjects or diminish their achievements is likely to arouse the reader's sympathy for them. Lytton Strachey's four Eminent Victorians have survived his debunking, and Strachey now seems less than any of them. Conversely, and paradoxically, however, the admiring but scrupulous biographer may provoke a contrary response from the reader. While the hostile biography may make us sympathetic to its victim, the admiring one, even when it stops well short of being an example of hagiography, may leave one liking its subject less than one had expected. So, to my surprise and dismay I found myself coming to dislike John Betjeman as portrayed in Bevis Hillier's masterly three volumes, even though Hillier wrote of him with admiration, sympathy and affection. Whereas the hostile biography leaves you thinking, 'yes this may be amusing, but it's not fair', the sympathetic one, offering an honest portrait of its subject, may disturbingly have you conclude, 'yes, I'm sure he has got X right, and I can see that he liked him; unfortunately I don't'.

STILL WITH US

1 NOVEMBER 2008

Chesterton refuses to go away. You may think he should have done
so. Orwell tried to show him the door:

> Chesterton was a writer of considerable talent who chose to suppress
> both his sensibilities and his intellectual honesty in the cause of Roman
> Catholic propaganda. In the last 20 years of his life ... every book that
> he wrote, every paragraph, every sentence, every incident in every story,
> every scrap of dialogue, had to demonstrate beyond possibility of mistake
> the superiority of the Catholic over the Protestant or the pagan.

Given that Orwell asserted that everything he himself wrote was
intended to advance the cause of democratic socialism, I'm not sure that
he was entitled to complain that others were writing propaganda, but of
course it was the nature of the propaganda and the tenor of Chesterton's
argument that he found offensive. Chesterton refused to believe in
the idea of progress and held the theology of St Thomas Aquinas in
higher regard than the science of Darwin or the philosophy of Marx
or Nietzsche. It's a mistake, he once wrote, to suppose that Shakespeare
had not thought of the Superman. He had; he just didn't think much
of him. That this dismissal may do scant justice to Nietzsche's concept is
beside my immediate point.

It is Chesterton's scepticism with regard to modernity that makes
what might seem his most timely book — *The Flying Inn* — read
very oddly. Most *Spectator* readers will doubtless recall its conceit,
which is that England has become a Muslim state, one in which
alcohol (though itself an Arabic word) is banned. Then, you may

remember, a Sussex innkeeper, an Irish adventurer and a charming girl set out on an exuberant course with a mobile inn, a barrel of rum, a great cheese, a dog called Quoodle, and a tendency to burst into song. This is all very jolly, but the oddity of the book is that the aristocratic converts to Islam adopt the religion on account of the appeal of its simplifying modernity, whereas nowadays those who, like the former *Spectator* contributor, Mark Steyn, seek to make our flesh creep with doleful prophecies of the Islamification of the member-states of the European Union, regard Islam as backward, stuck in the Middle Ages, and in its extremist form, as a jealous repudiation of modernity. In short, Chesterton's version of Islam does not at all accord with our experience of it. So *The Flying Inn* ought to be out-of-date. And yet Chesterton won't go away.

He is still very much with us. A French literary magazine, L'Atelier du Roman, has just devoted the greater part of its latest issue to him, with articles on *Anarchy in the Service of Orthodoxy (Vice Versa)*, *Inquest on Father Brown*, *Two or Three Things Learned from Chesterton*, *The Orthodoxy of an Everlasting Man*, *Science Fiction and Chesterton*, and *It was Better Before*, which last title might have made Orwell grind his teeth.

What is disconcerting for many about Chesterton is that, while deadly serious, he revelled in paradoxes, absurdity and farce. He believed in the Devil, believed in him as perhaps few in the last centuries did, but the weapon he employed against him was laughter; he was at one with Rabelais : 'the discovery of the reality of evil and the battle against it are at the basis of all gaiety and even of all farce'. Chesterton would have found Orwell admirable — and ridiculous; ridiculous because of his solemnity. 'The men who really believe in themselves are all in lunatic asylums', he declared.

He thought in paradoxes, on the sensible ground that if an idea is worth anything it ought to be able to be held upside down and shaken about. Sometimes, admittedly, the paradoxes flew too easily, too frequently and tiresomely from his pen. He wrote too much and often, I suspect, when he was tired, and then the paradoxes had a mechanical or tinkling sound like music from an elderly barrel-organ.

But at his best they make you think, and this is always disturbing: 'Reason is itself a matter of faith. It is an act of faith to assert that our thoughts have any relation to reality at all.' That's a thought you get your mind round. Because he was a man of faith he understood and valued doubt. He thought Charles II's deathbed admission to the Roman Church proof of his perfect scepticism. The wafer might, or might not be, the body of Christ, but then it might, or might not be, a wafer.

More than 70 years after his death he remains an entertaining writer, and a disquieting one. In the opinion of the editor of *L'Atelier du Roman*, Lakis Proguidis, 'no twentieth-century author has so thoroughly examined the yawning gulf cut in each soul by the ideology of Progress'.

AUTHOR! AUTHOR!

15 NOVEMBER 2008

Malcolm Lowry liked to quote the Spanish philosopher, Ortega y Gasset, who saw Man's life as a sort of novel, made up as you go along. Certainly there are times when life aspires to the condition of fiction. The story of Peter Mandelson, George Osborne, Nat Rothschild and the Russian oligarch might have been written by several novelists. Somerset Maugham, for instance, would have told it straight, dead-pan, through his favourite disillusioned, mildly cynical, narrator — old Mr Maugham himself, scarcely disguised — and would have presented it as an example of human folly. His focus would have been on Osborne, depicted as a callow young man of dangerous sincerity.

However, as the story unfolded in the newspapers — Osborne's account of the conversation with Mandelson in the Greek taverna, Rothschild's letter to *The Times*, the revelations of Mandelson's previous dealings with the oligarch — it seemed as if we were reading an episode from Simon Raven's *Alms for Oblivion* series. It had the familiar gamey Raven ingredients: betrayal of confidences, the desire for revenge, unfaithful friends. Money floated in the air, forever just out of reach of the English public-school product eager to get his hands on it. Only a sexual element was lacking, but Raven would have supplied it. Perhaps the Mandelson figure had taken a fancy to the youthful Osborne one as an undergraduate, charmed him, seduced him, and then abruptly dropped him? Something like that. Meanwhile the Rothschild character might himself be a discarded lover of the Tory politician and now besotted with the

Labour one. There ought to be a Greek boy somewhere, but I don't quite see where he is to be fitted in.

Then, though the Osborne character's disclosure of Mandelson's confidences should be provoked by pique and injured vanity, the set-up in a Raven novel would have been devised in order to discredit Osborne and the Tory party. Strings are pulled by sinister off-stage figures in the Security Services with the unsuspecting Rothschild as their puppet. They are working in mysterious collusion with the Russian oligarch, whom they are also blackmailing. Establishment figures rescue the hapless O, and then a busty, big-thighed woman takes over to keep him out of further trouble. In the Raven novel, as in life, the Mandelson character emerges unscathed, skating serenely over the thinnest of ice.

The Russian oligarch himself plays only a minor role in the Raven novel where he is a mere cardboard figure. Raven was seldom convincing with characters who had not been to an English public school and Cambridge. Indeed the *coup de foudre*, when M first catches sight of O, inevitably strikes at a dinner in Lancaster College, King's in all but name.

It would be very different if Trollope had written the novel. The sexual element would go. So would the secret services. No need for them at all. The O figure is now an outsider, like Phineas Finn, a young politician on the make, a man of good intentions but weak virtue, dazzled by wealth and corrupted by ambition. M is the spider weaving his web to entrap the innocent. His indiscretions in the taverna are calculated. The money O asked for — in the novel, if not in real life — is handed over in return for a bond to which O has put his name. So he is now in the clutches of the oligarch working with M to dish the Tory party's chances of winning the next election. As for R's letter to *The Times*, that is undoubtedly drafted by M, and R is compelled to put his name to it because of some dark secret in his life which M has discovered and threatens to reveal. Yet the oligarch's role remains murky. Perhaps it's not a Trollope novel after all.

If not Trollope, then who? Disraeli obviously. The story has all the ingredients of one of his glittering political romances: the idealistic 'Young England' Tory, the scion of a great Jewish house, the sinister foreigner whose dark ambitions are never fully disclosed (for any such disclosure would strain the reader's credulity), and at the heart of the novel the master-intriguer M, motivated less by malignity than by the sheer delight he takes in his ability to lure the innocent O to his doom. The novel would reek of great wealth, subject of fascination to one as habitually and heavily in debt as Disraeli. Almost every page would be enlivened by sparkling epigrams, such as may never fall from the lips of the originals, paradoxes and political maxims, and the denouement would be fantastic.

'When I want to read a novel, I write one,' Disraeli said, and it's a shame he is not still about to write this one. Mandelson certainly is a character who cries out for a novelist with his gifts.

SNOW AGAIN

13 DECEMBER 2008

Flying to Athens on one of his last visits to Greece, Simon Gray started reading a novel by C. P. Snow, one of those old orange Penguins. After 50 pages he 'still had no idea what the story was about'. It seemed foggy, 'but an odd sort of fog, everything described so clearly, and yet everything obscured ... he describes his world without seeing it, almost as if he thinks adjectives are in themselves full of detail and content.' As for the narrator, Lewis Eliot ('I suppose he's a front for old C. P. himself' — which he undoubtedly was), Simon remarked on his 'trick of having himself complimented' by other characters. This is certainly irritating.

The curious thing is that Simon wrote about this novel as if he had never read Snow previously. Yet surely he must have. Few under the age of, say, 40 may have read him, but back in the Fifties and Sixties I would be surprised if undergraduates who read novels had missed out on him. He was a considerable figure who got, for instance, a whole chapter to himself in *A Reader's Guide to the Contemporary English Novel* by Frederick R. Karl. An Associate Professor at the City University of New York, Karl describes Snow as 'a major literary figure', who 'returns the novel to a direct representation of moral, social and political issues'.

Well, I hadn't read anything by him for years, but the other day I too picked up an old Penguin: *The Sleep of Reason*, whose title is taken from one of Goya's etchings, '*The Sleep of Reason* brings forth monsters'. It's the second last novel in the *Strangers and Brothers* sequence which, back then, seemed to vie with Anthony Powell's

Dance as one of the most ambitious fictional ventures of the time.

'That afternoon I had been walking with my son in what for me were familiar streets, the streets of the town where I was born'. Quite a nice inviting opening. The hero, Eliot, has of course moved up in the world and away from this midland town (Leicester). But he returns occasionally because his father is still alive and because he has been elected a member of the University Court. The novel is set in the Sixties, and the first part deals principally with the case of four students (two couples) discovered having sex in the sitting-room of one of the women's hostels. It's all rather slow and laboured, and the full point becomes apparent only later. It is of course that times have changed, moral values are changing, self-restraint is going out of fashion, giving way to ideas of self-liberation. Eliot's old mentor, George Passant, described as a brilliant failure, has preached this to successive groups of disciples since Eliot himself was young. Instinct — being true to yourself — is to be more highly prized than reason.

The students' behaviour is symptomatic of this change. The second part of the novel shows it take a horrible form. A boy is kidnapped by two young women, one of them Passant's niece, the other the sister of one of the students. The child is tortured and then murdered, and we follow the course of the trial.

The Sleep of Reason was published in 1968, and the case and the novel obviously draw on the Moors Murders. Snow's wife, Pamela Hansford Johnson, attended the trial of Brady and Hindley and wrote a book, *On Iniquity*, in which she argued that the murders should be linked to the prevailing climate of permissiveness; and this, if not put so bluntly, is the argument of the novel too.

In one sense the book fails. Snow is incapable of comprehending the horror of the crime, or at least of conveying that horror to us. Eliot's attempt to understand the young women leave him with 'a sense of mystification that led into nothing.' He is, like his author, too much a man of the rational, ordered world. One thinks of what Dostoevsky or Simenon might have made of these two.

Yet there is something impressive in Eliot's lumbering, laborious efforts to comprehend something out of his experience, beyond his imagining. He is a conventional figure, whose success has enabled him to believe that the world is well-ordered. Somebody once ascribed to him the opinion of 'an elder statesman of science' that 'sensible men usually reached sensible conclusions'. He knows enough to think this 'an astonishing remark', not enough to understand a world from which that sort of sense has been banished.

All the same, there's more to old Snow than Simon allowed: a dogged honesty and an ability to show us the world as it presents itself to practical men engaged in public affairs, to show it in its strengths and limitations. Not enough to make a great novelist, but enough to make him a satisfyingly good one.

GETTING THE DETAIL RIGHT
10 JANUARY 2009

Evelyn Waugh told Nancy Mitford that he was 'surprised to find that Proust was a mental defective. He has absolutely no sense of time.' (Joke, given the novel's title?) 'He can't remember anyone's age. In the same summer as Gilberte gives him a marble and Françoise takes him to the public lavatory in the Champs Élysées, Bloch takes him to a brothel.'

Well, I can't remember just where this comes in *À la Recherche*, but suspect that either Waugh or Scott-Moncrieff, whose translation he was reading, made a confusion of tenses. Be that as it may, time is a problem for the novelist, especially one writing a *roman fleuve* published over the years in successive volumes, or one who employs the same character or characters in a number of books.

Agatha Christie, for instance, got herself into a mess with Hercule Poirot, though she never seemed to mind and sailed serenely on. All the same, on his first appearance in *The Mysterious Affair at Styles* (1917), old Papa Poirot, as he refers to himself there, has already retired from the Belgian police. So one may assume that he is over 60 at least. Yet he was still solving murders 50 years later.

Nobody, I suppose, minds about such oddities. Other novelists who aim at accuracy of representation may get into more serious difficulties. Even Anthony Powell, scrupulous in having friends check that he got things right, sometimes appears to have muddled his chronology.

In *A Buyer's Market* Mr Deacon's death (from a fall down the stairs of a nightclub) seems to have taken place no more than a matter of months after Jenkins encountered him at the coffee-stall by Hyde Park Corner and they went on to Milly Andriadis's party. Yet, when Jenkins meets him with Moreland and the music critics in the Mortimer at the beginning of *Casanova's Chinese Restaurant*, their 'renewed acquaintance' has evidently lasted longer. Jenkins remarks, for example, on the 'regular autumn exhalation of eucalyptus, or some other specific against the common cold (to which Mr Deacon was greatly subject)'. 'Regular' suggests years, rather than months. Is Jenkins's memory at fault, or did Powell find that, having killed Deacon off a couple of books previously, he had more use for him?

Again, the first sentence of *A Buyer's Market* is: 'The last time I saw any examples of Mr Deacon's work was at a sale, held obscurely in the neighbourhood of Euston Road, many years after his death.' Well, that novel was published in 1952. Twenty years later when Powell brought the sequence to a conclusion with *Hearing Secret Harmonies*, we learn that this isn't true. Deacon has been rediscovered as E. Bosworth Deacon and Barnabas Henderson stages a retrospective exhibition of his work in his new gallery, which Jenkins attends.

How to account for this discrepancy, not admittedly of any great importance? Had Powell forgotten the opening of *A Buyer's Market*, or did he not care that he was seemingly allowing Jenkins to contradict himself?

The answer may depend on just when we think that Jenkins is telling – or writing? – the story. Is he indeed writing it at all? Powell himself was vague when I asked him about this on a visit to The Chantry some 20 years ago. As far as I remember he said that he rather supposed Jenkins was sitting by his fireside reminiscing. I didn't find this satisfying, if only because Jenkins's manner and elaborate style are scarcely conversational; indeed they are highly, and enjoyably, literary. But I didn't pursue the matter, partly because I felt it would be bad manners to do so, since it seemed to me that Powell hadn't thought about this question at all. No good reason, you may say, why he should have done so.

Yet he had thought deeply about the structure of the long novel. Hence, his remark about putting down what he called 'markers', characters or incidents lightly touched on when they first appear, to be picked up and developed at a later stage in the narrative, one example being the shy undergraduate, Paul, briefly met in Sillery's rooms in *A Question of Upbringing*, not encountered again until the last volume when he reappears as Canon Fenneau at the Royal Academy dinner. Nevertheless one wonders how much was planning, how much happy chance. When at Stringham's wedding in *A Buyer's Market* we are told that 'little Pamela Flitton, who was holding the bride's train, felt sick at this moment, and rejoined her nurse at the back of the church,' did Powell already envisage her appearance as a 'femme fatale' in *The Military Philosophers* and later volumes? Did he already know that she would vomit into that large Chinese pot, so difficult to clean, after Erridge's funeral in *Books Do Furnish a Room?* I wish I knew.

WHY WRITE HISTORICAL NOVELS

9 MAY 2009

Amanda Craig recently rebuked her fellow novelists for avoiding the contemporary scene and setting their novels in the past. We should be more like the Victorians, she said, and have the courage to write about our own times. If the novel is to be relevant to readers, it should address today's issues. Why, she asked, is Hilary Mantel publishing a novel about Henry VIII's henchman, Thomas Cromwell, rather than ... Well, I don't recall if she actually suggested an alternative subject, but her point is clear. Writing historical novels is an evasion of the novelist's duty.

Of course Hilary Mantel has written novels set in the here and now, and very good ones. If she chooses to diversify and write one set in the sixteenth century, that's her business, and I should be surprised if her readers don't approve. Nevertheless Amanda Craig's charge is worth considering, even if her assertion seemed just a bit sweeping.

Comic novels, one should say, are almost always contemporary, because the foibles of one's own time are matter for the comic spirit. This has been the case, from Fielding and Austen, by way of Waugh and Powell, to Amis, father and son. Likewise novels of domestic life tend to be set in or near the immediate present.

It's when you are dealing with a public theme that difficulties arise. Set such a novel in the first decade of this century, and you are quite likely to end up with journalism, fictional journalism certainly, good journalism perhaps, but a work that is subject to the fate of almost all journalism, which is to be out of date very soon. In the last couple of years I have read half a dozen novels in which the events of 9/11 play a part, and none has been convincing. This is not due to lack of talent on the author's part; it's simply because 9/11 is too close in time to enable us to see it in perspective. It hasn't settled in the imagination; it hasn't yet been digested.

Novelists need time. Novels are made in part from recollection. This was as true of the Victorians as of writers today. Certainly Dickens was prepared to write about contemporary social conditions and abuses in, for example, *Hard Times*, not to my mind one of his best novels, though F. R. Leavis thought it was. But, though Dickens was living in the Railway Age, his characters usually travel by stagecoach. It is the world of his youth, even the world of his childhood, that he portrays most vividly. His rival Thackeray was a fine journalist, alert to changing fashions in manners and morals, but *Vanity Fair*, published in 1847, is set in and around 1815, the year of Waterloo. *Middlemarch* (1871) is one of the greatest of Victorian novels, but, in setting, it is pre-Victorian, treating of the agitation of society in the run-up to the Great Reform Bill of 1832. Only a couple of Scott's novels (*The Antiquary* and *St Ronan's Well*) are set in his own time; the half-dozen best of the Waverley novels deal with the Scotland of the century before he was born, while his greatest commercial success, Ivanhoe, goes back to the Middle Ages.

There are reasons why authors may choose to turn to the historical novel. The first is commercial. A good historical novel may sell better than a good contemporary one, and it may stay in print much longer. It is also perhaps more likely to be reprinted, simply because it doesn't date. A novel about Thomas Cromwell will probably be as interesting in 20 years as it is today. This isn't necessarily the case with a novel treating of what is immediately interesting in 2009.

Then novelists are always in danger of running out of material. Your own experience and your observation of the world around you may yield matter for perhaps only half a dozen novels. The more you write, the thinner the matter may be, and the more hours you spend at your desk, the fewer you spend out there in the world where material is to be gathered. But there is no dearth of matter in history. Reading will give you the stuff from which innumerable novels may be made. Your eye may not be as keen as when you were young, your ear not as alert, your receptiveness to new experience may have become dulled, but history offers you a rich choice of subjects.

Finally it gives you what all novelists seek — and often despair of finding: the outline of a plot. You still have to devise incident and dialogue, to flesh out characters and work up descriptions, but at least you know the road you are travelling. There are signposts along the way. You know you have to get Caesar to the theatre of Pompey on the Ides of March 44 BC. You know your destination. What a relief!

DELIGHT FADING

4 JULY 2009

'I think there would be something wrong with a middle-aged man who could take pleasure in Firbank.' That, more or less, was Evelyn Waugh's judgement in the interview he accorded the *Paris Review* in the mid-Fifties. (I say 'more or less' because I can't lay my hands on that volume of the interviews, but if the words are not exact, the sense is). Yet Firbank had, as he admitted, influenced him when young, along with Hemingway, who had also, as Waugh observed, developed 'the technical discoveries upon which Ronald Firbank so negligently stumbled'.

That quotation, unlike perhaps my first one, is accurate, for it is taken from an admiring essay on Firbank's work which Waugh wrote in 1929. He had reservations even then: 'His coy naughtiness about birches and pretty boys will bore most people with its repetition'; and he admitted that 'even among critics of culture and intelligence there will, no doubt, always be many to whom his work will remain essentially repugnant'. Nevertheless 'condemnation of him implies ... distaste for a wide and vigorous tendency in modern fiction'.

Though the young Waugh may himself have delighted in the naughtiness that such critics found repugnant, for his own homosexual phase was not long behind him, it was probably the simpering frivolity of Firbank's treatment of sex which came to irritate him in middle age. But his chief interest in 1929 was in what he called Firbank's 'technical peculiarities', which had enabled him to find a solution to 'the aesthetic problem of representation in fiction'. He had achieved 'a new, balanced interrelation of subject and form'. His later novels were 'almost devoid of any attributions of cause to effect; there is the barest minimum of direct description; his compositions are built up, intricately and with a balanced alternation of the wildest extravagance and the most austere economy, with conversational nuances'.

This, minus the 'wildest extravagances', was what Hemingway was also doing in his early short stories, which remain perhaps his best work, and it was what Waugh himself was to do in *Vile Bodies* and *Black Mischief*, with the wildest extravagances restored there. His debt to Firbank was considerable. 'In his dialogue there is no exchange of opinion. His art is purely selective.' These early Waugh novels are often called satires, and there is indeed a satirical element. But they are principally exercises in style. 'Exchange of opinion' is as rare in these novels as in Firbank's.

Waugh continued to maintain that he was not interested in an investigation of character, but regarded writing as 'an exercise in the use of language'; it was 'speech, drama, and events' that interested him. Doubtless this was true. Nevertheless, from *Brideshead* onwards, and most certainly in the *Sword of Honour* trilogy, one can see that themes and content have come to matter more to him. He is now as interested in what he has to say as in how he says it. The aesthete has not been suppressed by the moralist, but he is yoked to him.

In that Firbank essay he wrote of the novelist being 'fettered to cause and effect', just as 'in painting till the last generation the aesthetically significant activity of the artist had always to be occasioned by anecdote and representation' — precisely the kind of paintings that Waugh would collect in middle age. He had come by then a long way from the boy who wrote *In Defence of Cubism* and declared that 'the resemblance to life does not in the least concern the merits of the picture'.

It is natural, perhaps because it is reassuring, to suppose that one's taste improves, one's appreciation deepens and one's judgment becomes wiser as one grows older; natural to think that one becomes a better reader. Sometimes we may. In *How Fiction Works* James Wood says, 'I know from my own old books, wantonly annotated 20 years ago when I was a student, that I routinely underlined for approval details and images and metaphors that now strike me as commonplace, while serenely missing things which now seem wonderful.' No doubt this also is true. Yet, with the passing of time, a fresh and generous response to literature may be lost. If, for example, Aldous Huxley's *Antic Hay* now seems to me verbose, ponderous and too often tiresome, does this mean I am wiser than my 18-year-old self who found it entrancing? If Swinburne no longer delights as he did when I was young, does this signify that he is a lesser poet than I thought him then, or am I perhaps lesser than I was when the choruses of *Atalanta in Corydon* sent the spirit dancing? If poets, Swinburne among them, may deteriorate with age, perhaps we, as readers, may do so also? Was Waugh's 1929 delight in Firbank a sign of immaturity or is the middle-aged novelist's rejection of him evidence of a form of critical arteriosclerosis?

FAIRNESS TO WHOM?

8 AUGUST 2009

Between 1945 and his death in 1961 Ernest Hemingway published only two books, apart from collections of stories mostly written before the war. The two were *Across the River and Into the Trees* and *The Old Man and the Sea.* The first was generally considered a failure, the second a success; and it's doubtless perversity that makes me much prefer *Across the River.*

The meagre tally might suggest he was burned out, but for most of the time he was working hard on various projects, and the difficulty was to finish books. This was partly because the economy of his early work had given way to loquaciousness, and he went on and on, partly because his earnings from royalties, adaptations and occasional journalism were so high that he was free from the need of most authors to get work in print as soon as possible.

Five books, not including collections of short stories, journalism and letters, have been published since his death: *A Moveable Feast* (1964), *Islands in the Stream* (1970), *The Dangerous Summer* (1985), *The Garden of Eden* (1986), and *True at First Light* (1999). Since all were left unfinished, the form in which they have appeared owed much to editors who had to choose from different versions of the same passage and who cut heavily. Of the five books only *A Moveable Feast* and *The Garden of Eden* are, I would say, successes, but they are very considerable ones.

Now a new edition of the Paris sketches, *A Moveable Feast*, is being published by Scribner's in New York. The editor is Hemingway's grandson, Sean Hemingway, and he has made substantial changes.

Some chapters have been relegated to an appendix, and the last chapter, 'There Is Never Any End To Paris', appears in a very different form. Sean Hemingway believes that the 1964 version is unjust to his grandmother, Hemingway's second wife, Pauline, and does not represent his grandfather's true feelings. He insists that the book was left unfinished and asserts that the last chapter as published was cobbled together by Hemingway's widow, Mary, who had quarrelled with Pauline and wished to show her in a bad light. (Though Pauline herself had died as long ago as 1951.)

This claim has been rejected by A. E. Hotchner, Hemingway's friend, disciple, business and literary associate in the last dozen years of his life. Hotchner, in an article in the *New York Times*, insists that the 1964 book is very much the manuscript which he himself delivered to Scribner's in 1960, and that Mary had nothing to do with editing or, more importantly, reworking the last chapter. Hotchner is probably right. Nevertheless there is this to be said for Sean Hemingway's new version: that in April 1961 Hemingway wrote to Charles Scribner, Jr., to say that the Paris book couldn't be published in its present condition; it was unfair to Hadley (his first wife), Pauline and Scott Fitzgerald. But he also added that everything he had since done to the book had made it worse.

That this judgement was correct is, sadly, proved by the version of the final chapter edited by Sean Hemingway and also published in the *New York Times*. Certainly it shows both Hemingway and Pauline in a better light. She doesn't appear so selfishly unscrupulous and deceitful; he takes responsibility and blame for the break-up with Hadley more on himself. We no longer have only the picture of a determined woman breaking up his marriage while posing as his wife's best friend. Instead this is replaced by a tragic triangle, with Hemingway himself guilty and gnawed by remorse.

No doubt this is to his credit and offers a fairer and kinder picture of Pauline. Unfortunately the new version is garrulous instead of laconic and we miss what Wilfred Sheed called the appropriate moral poison, the malaise that, as [Edmund] Wilson says, undermines 'the sunlight and the green summer landscapes of *The Sun Also Rises*'.

The new version is full of explanations which weaken the impact, and which reek of self-pity. There is self-pity in the 1964 edition too, but it is concealed behind a mask of stoicism. It is nastier, but it is also artistically right. It is effective because in this version Hemingway was true to his own artistic credo: that you can leave anything out, so long as you know what it is you are omitting, and the work is stronger for doing so. 'I thought we were invulnerable again, and it wasn't until we were out of the mountains in late spring and back in Paris, that the other thing started again.' Cut. Now we have another sentence which dilutes the effect.

Sean Hemingway may have done his grandma justice — but it is at his grandfather's expense.

AN EDITOR'S INFLUENCE

7 NOVEMBER 2009

Way back in 1984 when I was editing, rather incompetently, the *New Edinburgh Review*, I published a story by Raymond Carver. It was entitled Vitamins. I can't remember how much I knew about Carver then, or even how the manuscript arrived on my desk. Probably it was sent by his agent, and was taken from a new collection, *Cathedral*, which was to be published by Collins. It is a good story — I've just read it again — and less minimalist than some of the work by which he made his name.

Which is very much to the point, for it seems that these stories owed a great deal to his editor, Gordon Lish, and that Carver himself was not entirely happy, to put it mildly, with Lish's surgery which cut some stories by half, or even more than that.

'Even though they may be closer to works of art than my original,' he wrote to Lish, 'they're still apt to hasten my demise.' In short, the style, with its abrupt transitions and unspoken sentences, which came to be called Carveresque, might more accurately have been termed Carver-Lish or Carver-Lite. In the collection which Carver called *Beginners* and Lish re-titled *What We talk About When We Talk About Love*, it wasn't only cuts that were made. In one story a man murders a woman in Carver's original version, two women in the published one.

Now Carver's second wife Tess Gallagher, whom he met when he was no longer a 'practising alcoholic' and with whom he lived for the last dozen years of his life, has brought out a new edition of these stories, with the original title *Beginners* which she claims is the book as Carver himself wrote it, before Lish got to work on it.

Criticism of what Lish did to Carver — or perhaps for him? — has been about for years, provoking him in 1998 to dismiss his author as a 'mediocrity' whom he had made famous. He later retracted this comment, but it may well have represented his true opinion. It would be quite understandable if he believed that his editorial work had improved the stories and so made Carver's reputation. Conversely, it is equally understandable if Carver resented this, preferred the stories as he had written them, and even felt there was something false about the esteem in which he came to be held.

The story of Carver and Lish and the publication now of the Lish-less edition of the stories raise a number of points, none of which is easy to answer satisfactorily.

The first concerns the proper relationship of author to editor. Some authors, Iris Murdoch for one, have refused to be edited at all. Like Yahweh, they declare 'what I have written, I have written'. If they are authors of a certain standing, then they are likely to be able to override any editorial suggestions. Neither Evelyn Waugh nor Muriel Spark would have submitted to an editor as poor Carver did to Gordon Lish. On the other hand there are authors of a different type, who are less sure about what they want to say than Waugh and Spark were. William Golding was one such. John Carey's biography shows just how often he was uncertain about the way a book was going, and how much he relied on his editor at Faber, Charles Monteith, to offer helpful suggestions when he had read the first draft of a novel.

Second, we may ask to what extent credit for a heavily edited book belongs to the author. Now that so many bestsellers, both fiction and non-fiction, are ghost-written, such a question may seem absurd. But it matters to a real author — clearly it mattered a great deal to Carver. He felt that his work had been taken away from him and that there was something spurious about the reputation it won him. Was he his own man or had Lish stolen his identity and foisted a false one on him? The answer must surely depend on whether the author feels that he remained in control of his book. You can use editors without losing possession of your work, just as Dumas used collaborators to do research and sketch in outlines, and Renaissance painters employed apprentices to work on the simpler parts of a picture.

Finally is Tess Gallagher justified in publishing *Beginners* as Carver wrote it before the book was 'improved' by Lish? The answer is surely 'yes', because she knows Carver was unhappy with the Lish version. Admittedly the original one may do some damage to Carver's standing. It may make him seem a less remarkable and more ordinary writer. But reading the stories as he wrote them should be of interest, and some may seem better than in the Lish edition. I suspect Lish had no hand in *Vitamins* which I published so many years ago, and, reading it again, I still find it impressive. The only thing to regret is the poor standard of my own proof-reading.

WRITING OF, OR FROM, YOUR-SELF

30 JANUARY 2010

'All literature is, finally, autobiographical', said Borges. 'Every autobiography becomes an absorbing work of fiction', responded H. L. Mencken, though not, you understand, directly. Certainly the fictional element in autobiography is evident; Trollope thought that nobody could ever tell the full truth about himself, and A. S. Byatt has said that 'autobiographies tell more lies than all but the most self-indulgent fiction'. An exaggeration, perhaps, but one with a kernel of truth.

Borges's remark must, however, set any novelist pondering. In the most immediate sense it appears to be untrue. 'What about invention?' we may cry, 'what about the imagination?' Moreover, we have all read, and delighted in, novels that seem to have had no connection with the author's life. Yet one should never discount sense in any observation from Borges. So what did he mean?

We can all see that many novels which don't appear to be autobiographical may nevertheless have been born in their author's fantasy life. Ian Fleming never had James Bond's adventures, but Bond is surely a projection of Fleming as, in certain moods, he would have liked to be. Anyone seeking a real-life model for Bond other than Fleming himself is surely wasting their time.

On the other hand, novelists resent, quite naturally, the suggestion that they draw only from their own lives. It's patently absurd. Nobody, after all, supposes that a crime novelist like P. D. James or Ruth Rendell is a murderer, however many corpses litter their novels. It would be ridiculous to suggest that any of these murders represented some sort of wish-fulfilment, or 'displaced activity'. Likewise, it would make little sense to identify Lady James with Adam Dalgliesh or Lady Rendell with her Chief Inspector Wexford.

In one of her novels — *Loitering with Intent* or *A Far Cry from Kensington*, I can't recall which — Muriel Spark has her narrator remark that, while some people say that nothing happens to them, everything happens to the novelist. Taken literally, this is nonsense. Nothing happens to most novelists a good deal of the time. They sit at their desk, a notebook in hand, or before a typewriter or computer, and, if work is going well, may not even look out of the window to observe life going by. Novelists, by and large, lead retired lives, and, if they don't, then they usually write fewer and probably worse novels. What happens to them happens in their mind, their memory and their imagination.

And this surely is where we return to Borges. Novelists certainly draw on their experience, and that experience includes their observation of other people. Such observation leads to speculation. V. S. Pritchett would look at a couple and ask himself, 'what does she see in him?', and from the question, a story would be spun. But it would be Pritchett's story, made in his imagination from a brief glimpse of the material offered him. The couple in question might never recognise themselves.

Experience is itself of two sorts. There is the experience we have lived in what we call 'real life', though this will usually be altered or amended in memory. Then there is the alternative experience, the route which we did not take, but might have taken, the fork in the road we turned aside from. We can imagine that journey and make fiction of it. The novel that emerges may be considered a piece of counter-factual autobiography. We explore the past we turned away from.

Borges may have meant something simpler. If you want to know a novelist — or poet or playwright — read his novels or poems or plays, not a biography. This makes very obvious sense. Even the best biographies track the man or woman revealed in their social life, a being very different, as Proust argued in his reproof of the critic Sainte-Beuve, from the one who wrote. In discussing Stendhal, Sainte-Beuve made much of the memories of those who had known him. Proust found this absurd. 'For those friends, the self which produced the novels was eclipsed by the other, which may have been very inferior to the outer selves of many other people.' What the writer gives to the world is, Proust thought, 'the secretion of one's innermost life, written in solitude'.

And it is this secretion of the writer's innermost life which makes literature autobiographical. You come to know, say, Graham Greene much more fully, and truly, from reading *Brighton Rock*, *The Heart of the Matter* or *The Honorary Consul* than from the fat volumes of Norman Sherry's biography, which offer the fruit of years of assiduous research. Equally, Dickens is brought to life in Great Expectations much more vividly than any biographer has ever managed to do. It couldn't, really, be otherwise.

A RACE WELL RUN

6 MARCH 2010

More than 20 years ago I wrote an admiring article about Dick Francis. I made, if I recall, only one mild criticism: that he sometimes piled a bit too much misfortune on his damaged heroes. There was, for instance, the novel in which the narrator's wife was in an iron lung and the villains put pressure on him to abandon his investigation by invading her bedroom and threatening to switch off the electric current that kept her alive. This was going a bit far, I suggested. A couple of weeks later I got a charming letter from Francis thanking me for all the nice things I had written, and then saying that as a matter-of-fact his wife Mary had spent some time in an iron lung, and he had found himself wondering 'what if…?' 'What if?' is the perfect kick-off for a novel of suspense.

Actually I was wrong about the damaged heroes of Francis's early novels. Giving them a flaw or some sort of psychological impairment made them more interesting, more convincing because more vulnerable. Sid Halley, former champion steeplechase jockey, had lost a hand and was horribly conscious of his disability, terrified when the villain in (I think) the second of the Halley novels threatened to smash his other hand. Daniel Roke, in *For Kicks*, was dissatisfied with his dutiful life in Australia, even though it took some horrible experiences to make him realise the attraction danger held for him. Philip Nore, in *Reflex*, is embittered by his grandmother's rejection of his beautiful feckless mother who died a heroin addict.

Robbie Finn, the hero of *Nerve* — perhaps the best of the 40 or so novels — feels himself an outsider, the only non-musical member of a family of famous musicians. His drive to succeed as a jockey is clearly compensation. *Nerve* is particularly interesting because Francis made the villain a mirror image of his hero: all his family are big shots in the horse world, but as a child he was afraid of horses and developed asthma to excuse his fear. Now a successful racing journalist, with a TV show which is a 'must' for everyone in racing, his jealousy of successful jockeys has unbalanced him. In his obsession he sets out to destroy their careers. *Nerve* is so good partly because Maurice is Francis's most complicated villain, even oddly sympathetic because he seems the hero's dark shadow-side.

If the later novels weren't quite as gripping as the early ones, it was not because Francis's imagination grew duller, or the pace of the narrative slackened (though that did happen in some books), but because his heroes tended to be super-competent, rather than damaged, capable not only of overcoming the villains but of putting everybody else's life to order as they did so. The hero of *10lb Penalty*, for instance, though barely out of school, not only sees off the villains in best Francis style, but also masterminds his father's political campaign. So, while one was always on the side of the damaged heroes, in the later books I occasionally entertained the unworthy thought that I would like to see these rather self-satisfied fellows taken down a peg or two.

Nevertheless, even the weakest of the novels were enjoyable. All the books were written with authority, in the first person, a method which carries conviction. The research was thorough — mostly, it seems, the work of Mary Francis. So there was a solidity of background which gave ballast to the story. Naturally the racing world was vividly and persuasively realised, but you could also learn quite a lot about merchant banking from Banker, photography from *Reflex*, rifle-shooting from *Twice Shy*, and air transport from *Flying Finish*. Then Francis had the ability, which is usually instinctive and denied to many novelists, to modulate pace. He knew when to slow the narrative and when to quicken it, and he was very good at domestic interludes, though it was strange that his characters always seem to drink instant coffee. The prose was plain, never drawing attention to itself, an ideal narrative style.

Finally the morality was satisfying. The good ended happily and the bad unhappily; which, as Wilde observed, 'is what fiction means'. Violence was always suffered by the hero and his associates, almost never gratuitously inflicted by him, though the revenge taken by Robbie Finn in *Nerve* was sufficiently unpleasant to be disturbing. In general, however, there was an old-fashioned and agreeable decency about all the novels; and in this they truly reflected the character and attitudes of their author. Few writers of our time can have given pleasure to more people. One always opened a new book by Dick Francis with a lively expectation of enjoyment, and the expectation was only rarely disappointed. He did what he set out to do, and did it very well. That is no mean achievement.

E. M. FORSTER
AND FRANK KERMODE
10 APRIL 2010

Any follower of literary blood sports should take a look at a review in the *Weekly Standard*, a conservative American magazine. You can find it on a site called *Arts & Letters*, which my son obligingly bookmarked for me. The present edition — at least I suppose it is the present one, not that it matters, since I understand that you can use the internet to summon articles from the vasty deep of time past — features the review, by Joseph Epstein of Sir Frank Kermode's 2007 Clark Lectures devoted to E. M. Forster. Forster's own book, *Aspects of the Novel*, had its origins in the same Cambridge lectures.

Epstein has armed himself with a two-barrelled shotgun, one barrel for Kermode, the other for Forster, whom he admits to having admired in his youth.

Kermode is gunned down first as a timid and conventional critic, incapable of offering anything but received opinion. We are reminded how quickly he abandoned his editorship of *Encounter* as soon as its ultimate source of funding (from the CIA) was revealed. Some may think this honourable, and certainly I doubt, given Sir Frank's immense distinction, if it would have occurred to many of us that 'he vacated his editorship faster than a preacher with an underage boy departing a bordello under police raid'.

Epstein explains Kermode's 'timidity' by his struggle to break through the English class barrier. Consequently, he has always been careful to 'sit on the right side of the fence'. Well, perhaps, though it may be that as an American Epstein's view of the English class barrier is just a bit out-dated — and was so even when Kermode was a young man. After all, one can think of academics rising from what used to be called 'humble backgrounds', who shattered that barrier and continued to lay about them with zest and indignation.

Having had his fun with Kermode, Epstein directs the other barrel at Forster, the liberal hero. Bloomsbury, he tells us, may have laid great emphasis on the importance of personal relations, but it set a pretty poor example of how to conduct them. 'It would be difficult, not at all incidentally, to find a group of people who betrayed one another more — sexually and in other ways — than the Bloomsbury Group.' This is splendid stuff, despite the ugly repetition of the word 'group', though one might add that they don't seem to have taken the sexual betrayals to heart; all part of the great game of personal relations, as it were.

Epstein has the usual go at Forster's remark about how, faced with the choice, he hoped he would have the courage to betray his country rather than his friend. Orwell dealt with that line long ago, rather more effectively. All the same, Forster raised a real question worth discussing rather that dismissing out of hand, one indeed which a few years later was to give Elizabeth Bowen the theme for that very fine novel, *The Heat of the Day*. The question of betrayal or treason is more complicated than appears at first sight. One natural response is denial, American liberals refusing to admit that Alger Hiss had indeed been a Soviet agent.

Then it's the turn of the novels, those half-dozen delicate works which have had Forster hailed 'as the great writer he most distinctly isn't'. Epstein now suspects that his own youthful admiration for them derived from his 'ardent desire to be among the sensitive, the considerate and the plucky' whom Forster extolled, claiming that there was 'a secret understanding between them when they meet' — a line inviting the old sneer, 'takes one to know one'. Epstein, soured perhaps by discovering that the novels are not what he once thought them, lets loose again: 'There is much evidence that in life, if not in his novels, Forster was insensitive, inconsiderate and schmucky.' Perhaps he was; Simon Raven called him a mean old thing when refused what he euphemistically called a loan. But of course this has nothing to do with the novels. Dickens was a bad husband. So what?

Apart from enjoying Epstein's attack, uninhibited in the manner of eighteenth-century Grub Street, and delivered without regard for any literary equivalent of the Queensberry Rules, I find that my opinion of Forster's novels is now no higher than his. When, not long ago, I re-read *A Passage to India*, I was irritated by the author's partiality. So I nod my head in agreement when Epstein declares that 'Forster, in the way he designed his novels, was playing with loaded dice.' Quite so, I say, and yet, here I pause. I thought them marvellous when I was young. Can I be sure my judgment now is wiser than my judgment was then? Have the novels deteriorated, or have I?

THE LIVES OF OTHERS

8 MAY 2010

'My wife doesn't understand me,' the man said to his Jewish psychoanalyst. 'I should be so lucky!' was the reply. It's a common complaint, not being understood. Yet surely only the most shameless would like others to know us exactly as we are or as we know ourselves. This is one reason some writers shrink from the prospect of having their Life written. Kipling called biography 'the higher cannibalism', and tried to pre-empt one by writing his own decidedly reticent memoir, *Something of Myself*. Something indeed, but not a lot. Subsequently, his widow, Carrie, burned letters and other papers; their daughter, Elsie, suppressed Frederick Birkenhead's biography without giving a reason, and when at last consenting to one, tied its author Charles Carrington's hands. One sees their point. In life Kipling concealed everything but his opinions; why should a biographer be free to expose what had been kept hidden from view.

Thomas Hardy, equally shy of the world's gaze, adopted a different stratagem. He wrote his own biography, to be published posthumously under his wife's name. The device failed to choke off the higher cannibals. He has repeatedly attracted the attention of biographers. We know much more about Hardy than he wished to be known.

Auden went further:

> Most genuine artists would prefer that no biography be written. A great deal of what passes for scholarly research is an activity no different from reading somebody's private correspondence when he is out of the room,

and it doesn't really make it morally any better if he is out of the room because he is in his grave.

This is Auden in his best pontifical vein. Yet he must have known that he would himself be the subject of a biography, and indeed his friend Charles Osborne wrote a frank and sympathetic one only a few years after the poet's death. Did this have Auden birling in the grave? Somehow I doubt it. He might, I suppose, have been more offended if no one had thought his Life worth writing.

Many, probably most, authors accumulate piles of paper. They keep diaries or notebooks. They write, and receive letters, often copying their own, and file them or stuff them into drawers and boxes. I would guess that many now print e-mails, both those they send and those which arrive in their inbox. If a tempting offer comes, they sell their papers to a university library, usually an American one. Those who attract no such offer sigh for one, in the hope that it might repair their bank balance, provide for their old age, and secure their posthumous fame.

'So long as men can breathe or eyes can see,/ So long lives this, and this gives life to thee'. '*Exegi monumentum aere perennius*'. Poets were once content to believe that their verses alone would bring them immortal fame. Now perhaps they are less certain, for we must all now be aware of our inheritance: the Great Unread. Who now reads Spenser or Dryden except university professors and, perhaps, their reluctant students? If you wish to be remembered for even one generation after you are dead, appoint a biographer and make sure he has material sufficient for a fat book.

And yet how inadequate most biography is, how inevitably inadequate. It is all right, as Auden remarked, for a man of action — 'a ruler, a statesman, a general', for in his case 'the man is identical with the biography'. His or hers was a public life, and that may indeed be satisfactorily written. Much, of course, will be omitted, for even rulers, statesmen and generals have private, and happily hidden, lives. Moreover, they have, or may have, their secret life of the imagination, which they must often wish to take undisclosed to the grave.

The case of the artist is different. There is a gulf between the life lived from day to day, and the work done. The relationship between life and works is, Auden wrote, 'at one and the same time too self-evident to require comment — every work of art is, in one sense, a self-disclosure — and too complicated ever to unravel'.

This is surely true, and if the artist reveals himself in his work, he does so either unconsciously, often realising only years later how much he had given away, or he continues to hide behind a mask. He wants to be known and yet remain unknown, and the more subtle and scrupulous the artist, the more likely it is he will evade any biographer. Inasmuch as the biographer offers no more than the 'higher gossip' (which is the form cannibalism takes today), the artist distrusts and despises him; and yet, such is the longing for posthumous fame — fame of which he will sadly remain ignorant — that he will arrange to make materials available for a biography; or even, like Beerbohm's Enoch Soames, sell his soul to the devil. And who knows? He may bring off the desired double: to be remembered but still escape full understanding.

THE HELL OF WORKING
3 JULY 2010

Joseph Conrad was 38, more than halfway through his life, when his first novel, *Almayer's Folly*, was published in 1895. He died in 1924 with more than 30 books to his name. A good enough rate of production, you might think. An astonishing one actually, if you are to believe him. 'Full three weeks,' he wrote to his friend Galsworthy in 1911, '— no consecutive ideas, no six consecutive words to be found anywhere in the world. I would prefer a red hot gridiron to that cold blankness.'

The gloom wasn't new: 'The sight of a pen and an inkwell fills me with anger and horror.' Or again:

> I sit down for eight hours every day and sitting down is all. In the course of that working day of eight hours I write three sentences which I erase before leaving the table in despair.

As his friend Ford Madox Ford remarked with characteristic insouciance, 'Conrad spent a day finding the *mot juste*; then killed it.' Nevertheless the books got written; and it seems improbable that Conrad would have exchanged the struggle against which he inveighed for the facility that allowed Edgar Wallace to dictate a novel over a weekend. Still one feels he must often have resented Ford who would play a few games of patience and then reel off a couple of thousand words, with the same apparent ease that he engaged in conversation. Very good words too.

It's a matter of temperament, I suppose. There are writers who would not be happy if the stuff came easily. They couldn't believe it was any good. Suffering the agony of creation is for them a necessary part of the game. How Conrad must have growled if he read Trollope's autobiography:

> I finished on Thursday the novel I was writing. On Friday I started another. Nothing really frightens me but the idea of enforced idleness. As long as I can write books, even though they be not published, I think I can be happy.

And as for Wodehouse, Conrad would have howled, as he did when his gout was bad, to read this: 'I love writing. I never feel really comfortable unless I am either actually writing or have a story going.'

None of this proves anything, which is always an agreeable reflection. The ease or difficulty of writing has nothing to do with the quality of the work. In any case, given that imaginative writers are by the nature of the trade liars, one should always greet anything they say about their work with some scepticism. William Faulkner for example spoke of the writer's 'dream', and said, 'it anguishes him so much he must get rid of it. He has no peace until then. Everything must go by the board.'

Well, Faulkner is a great novelist, perhaps the greatest of American novelists, but when he speaks of this 'anguish', it sits ill with the impression his best work conveys, which is that you are listening to a story told in rambling but cunning style, going back and forward in time, by a man in a rocking-chair on the porch of his house with a jug of corn liquor by his side and a good cigar in his mouth.

For many it's the getting down to work that is the problem. Few of us are as happily formed as Scott or Trollope, both of whom rose with the lark and got straight to their work (though Scott described his as his 'task'). Some will do almost anything, pleasant or unpleasant as the case may be, in order to put off the moment when they have to settle at their desk and confront the blank sheet or screen.

Hemingway recommended that when you are working on a novel you should start the working day by reading over what you have already written, or the last few chapters at least. Good advice, this, especially the qualification, for you could scarcely expect Tolstoy to read over all there was so far of *War and Peace* before settling to write, say, chapter 55. In theory, and often in practice, reading what you have already written gets you into the mood, the right vein, and so enables you to continue. That's fine if it reads well. But what if the prose seems leaden, the characters dim and the action slow? What do you do then? Blame it on your mood this morning and hope it may read better tomorrow? Or howl like a dog? Probably the best thing is to remember that at some stage in the writing of a novel, it has always seemed a mistake, but you have to keep on going and you may find, as you did in the past, that after all things come right.

THE JOY OF LIGHT VERSE

26 MARCH 2011

When cares attack, and life seems black,
How sweet it is to pot a yak,
Or puncture hares or grizzly bears,
And others I could mention;
But in my animal Who's Who
No name stands higher than the gnu,
And each new gnu that comes in view
Receives my prompt attention.

Wodehouse, of course, as I am sure all Spectator readers won't need to be told, from one of the Mulliner stories as I remember, and a perfect snatch of light verse, witty and dancing.

Just what constitutes light verse is no more easy to define than to decide what separates verse from poetry. Auden included Kipling's *Danny Deever* in an anthology of light verse, though a poem about a military execution might seem rather to belong to a book of grim verse. This is not so much because of the subject matter as the tone. Light verse can certainly treat of the dark side of things, but does so light-heartedly; witness Harry Graham's *Ruthless Rhymes* or Housman's ditty about a rather nasty rail accident which begins, '"Hallelujah" was the only observation/ That escaped Lieutenant-Colonel Mary Jane.'

Light verse may require more talent than poetry. Certainly it demands a high level of craftsmanship. The metrical skill displayed by Barham in his *Ingoldsby Legends* is beyond that of which many admired modern poets are capable — no names, no pack drill, though some highly esteemed ones come to mind. *Old Possum's Book of Practical Cats* is a more remarkable example of linguistic dexterity than *Four Quartets*, though the *Quartets* may be great poetry and *Possum* is playing with words and fancy.

Good light verse sticks in the memory almost unbidden. You have to work to get a passage from, say, *The Prelude* or *Paradise Lost* by heart, but light verse, even when it is not written for the musical theatre by the likes of Cole Porter and Noel Coward, and has therefore no accompanying tune, lodges itself in the mind with a dancing rhythm.

Of course the distinction between light verse and poetry is often blurred. *Don Juan* is a very great poem, with passages of sublime beauty, but much of it is light verse, like Byron's recipe for dealing with a hangover that begins: 'Ring for your valet, bid him quickly bring/ Some hock and soda water.' Very good advice too, as I recall from my own drinking days...

The nineteenth century was the great age of light verse, partly, I would suppose, because most who wrote it had received a classical education, and had been required to put passages of English into Latin, or indeed Greek, verse. Nobody would have pretended that the result was poetry, though it may occasionally have been that, but the exercise taught pupils about rhythm and the weighting of words. Once you had learned to write Latin hexameters that scanned correctly, you had acquired skills which were easily transferred to the writing of English verse. When you wonder at the virtuosity Kipling displayed in his mastery of metre and rhythm, remember that his favourite poet was Horace.

Children are still, I hope, brought up on Belloc's *Cautionary Verses*, which A. N Wilson, in his excellent biography, called 'technically faultless' with 'not a syllable out of place, not an epithet which could be improved'. This indeed is a judgment which might be applied to all really good light verse. Yet beside the *Cautionary Verses* should be placed *The Modern Traveller*, a long poem remarkable for its mastery of tone, wit and inventiveness:

And yet I really must complain
About the Company's champagne!
This most expensive kind of wine
In England is a matter
Of pride or habit when we dine
(Presumably the latter).
Beneath an equatorial sky
You must consume it or you die;
And stern indomitable men
Have told me, time and time again,
'The nuisance of the tropics is
The sheer necessity of fizz'.

It flows so easily — the verse, not the fizz — that you may be excused for thinking it came easily. Perhaps it did, but, if so, it was as a result of many hours of reading and verse-making.

Light verse is not dead. Betjeman, James Michie, Kingsley Amis, Gavin Ewart and Wendy Cope have all written delightful stuff — contributors to *The Spectator*'s weekly competition likewise, itself for years indeed set and judged by James Michie.

Yet there is, I fear, less good light verse than there was; fewer poets deviate into it, partly perhaps because much well-regarded modern poetry is written without the technical mastery which light verse demands, partly doubtless because few of them have been set to composing Latin hexameters. If the 'free schools' now in the process of being established set more of their pupils to learning Latin, there may be a revival of light verse and we could cry 'Hallelujah' without incurring the unhappy fate of Salvation Army Captain Mary-Jane who 'tumbled off the platform in the station/ And was cut in little pieces by the train'.

CHARACTERS OUT
OF CONTROL

13 APRIL 2011

Nabokov insisted he was in control of his characters. If he wanted them to cross the road, they jolly well did so. He had no time for writers who say that their character went his own way. Nevertheless his adored Pushkin reportedly said, 'Do you know, my Tatiana has rejected my Eugene. I never expected it of her.' It's possible of course that Nabokov's denial of his characters' autonomy was a piece of showing-off, possible also that his characters would have been livelier if he hadn't kept them on so short a leash. Pushkin, on the other hand, may have been making a joke, but more likely was expressing honest surprise. Characters should sometimes surprise their authors both in what they do and what they say. If they are to have any vitality, they should be more than puppets.

Novelists sometimes begin a book with only a vague idea of where it is heading, and with no knowledge of their full cast. Writing about that fine early novel *England Made Me* Graham Greene remarked how he 'had lived with one character, Anthony, for many years. He was an idealised portrait of my elder brother Herbert, and I had myself shared many of his experiences... Then suddenly the boat listed when Minty stepped on board. He was completely unexpected when he emerged from the pre-conscious – this remittance man who woke up one morning in his Stockholm lodgings watched by a spider under a tooth-glass'. Minty would 'steal all the scenes' in which he appeared. Greene 'resented him but couldn't keep him down'. Evidently Minty crossed the road when he felt like it, not when Greene told him to.

181

Sometimes one happens on a character by serendipity. There's a Swedish boy in a novella I wrote about the last days of Klaus Mann. It was a horrible wet morning and Klaus had emerged miserable and shaking from the little hotel where he was staying. So I took him – let him go? – to a bar. The Swedish boy's arrival there was as much of a surprise to me as to Klaus. I certainly hadn't expected him, but as soon as he was there, I knew he was needed; it was clear that he must seek to borrow money and, more importantly, that he could represent what Klaus wanted but couldn't have – not only the boy himself but a future. When the next day, I think, he walked out of the book with his girlfriend, I didn't know, or indeed care, where he was going or whether they would stay together. Probably they wouldn't but it didn't matter; he had done his work.

One might go further and argue that the more thoroughly you have imagined a character before you write, the more clearly you have mapped out the path he must follow, the more difficult it may be to breathe life into him. Of course you should have some sense of direction and some sense of the characters you will accompany on the journey. Of course too you may find that they are taking, or are in danger of taking, the wrong turning, and then, for the sake of the book's structure, you must haul them back. Quite often however it is wise to let them have their head, and trust them to go somewhere interesting. Novels are made more by instinct and luck, than by taking thought. When Pushkin expresses his surprise at Tatiana's rejection of Eugene, he is acknowledging her autonomy. Likewise I have always relished the story of Balzac turning from some tiresome discussion – about politics or his finances, I can't remember which – and saying, 'Now let's speak of important matters: who should Eugenie Grandet marry?' Clearly he didn't know the right answer, but the right answer would in time transpire.

Sometimes the author goes wrong, perhaps because he listens to advice from others. The end of *Great Expectations* is a notorious example. Dickens knew that there was no possible redemption for Estella – he had written her too truly for this to be possible; but, at the behest of either Wilkie Collins or Bulwer-Lytton – again I forget which – he gave the book a happy ending, and in doing so came close to ruining his masterpiece. He jerked Estella out of the course her life was taking and made her cross the road to an incredible domestic bliss. As Nicholas Freeling wrote: 'Men, always intolerably self-indulgent on the subject of fallen women, may accept this new sweet-and-sexy Estella; no woman can, does, or ever will.' Dickens should have had the artistic good sense to follow his instinct, and let her go. Instead he ruined his ending to save her from ruin – a piece of depressing sentimentality.

KING LEAR'S WIFE
31 OCTOBER 2011

Gordon Bottomley, Georgian poet with an unpoetic name, wrote a play called *King Lear's Wife*. I have never read it. *The Oxford Companion to English Literature* says he hoped to inspire a poetic revival in the theatre and that it is among the most successful of his plays. It might be interesting to see it revived. Or perhaps not. Most nineteenth and twentieth-century attempts at verse-drama proved forgettable.

Nevertheless Bottomley surely happened on an interesting subject, though one which critics of the school of Leavis would deplore, as they deplored A. C. Bradley's book on Shakespearean tragedy. L. C. Knights in a famous – once famous? – essay, 'How Many Children Had Lady Macbeth?' – poured scorn on the practice of treating Shakespearean characters as if they were real people with an anterior life beyond the play. Yet surely it is tempting to do so. When Lady Macbeth says she would have killed Duncan herself if he hadn't resembled her father as he slept, it's natural to wonder about her relationship with Dad.

As for King Lear's wife, we may suspect she had a hard time of it, Lear a domestic tyrant, the kind of husband who tells his wife that she can't possibly wear a revealing dress on a public occasion. In his own household, in his prime, we can be sure that his word was Law. Clearly all three daughters resented this – even Cordelia, who defies him by refusing to pretend that she loves him more than a daughter should love her father, to the exclusion, that is, of her future husband. As for Goneril and Regan it is clear that they despise him and dislike him. They display their contempt in their protestations of love, which they know that the old fool will accept as his due, and one would guess that apart from the advantage they expect from their lies, they take pleasure in deceiving him. Their subsequent treatment of Lear, and the relish they take in humiliating him, is evidence of their deep dislike. It's reasonable to suggest that this in part inspired by their sympathy for their bullied mother. Certainly they savour their revenge – revenge perhaps for an unhappy childhood.

It may be objected that any attempt to make sense of the two 'wicked daughters' is futile. They are mere conveniences. Shakespeare does not pretend to account for their hatred of their father. It's enough for the purpose of the play that they should display it. Finding a psychological explanation for their cruelty is self-indulgent. They are like the juvenile delinquents in Noel Coward's song: 'Waste no time on the wherefores and whys of it,/ We like crime, and that's about the size of it.' Even so, it's tempting to wonder. Does an actress playing Goneril or Regan try to understand the character, or should she be content merely to speak the lines? And certainly to do so without any thought of King Lear's wife?

In his comedies Shakespeare usually fights shy of a study of marriage. Like Jane Austen's novels, they end at the church door. There is admittedly a nice study of a married couple in *A Midsummer Night's Dream*, and if the female parts in his plays had been played by women rather than boy-actors, one might think that Oberon and Titania were based on a celebrated theatrical couple, joined in stardom and rivalry.

Marriage does feature in the tragedies, rarely happily. Antony and Cleopatra may be great lovers, but marriage destroys Antony, turning the great general into 'a strumpet's fool'. It does for Othello, another general, too. His emotional immaturity making him a jealous and impossible husband. There is some evidence that the Macbeths were once a happy couple – perhaps drawn together by the loss of however many children Lady Macbeth may have had. Certainly there is pain in Macbeth's cry to the doctor, 'Canst thou not minister to a mind diseased?' (Theme for a novel: Anne Hathaway's nervous breakdown and the strain put on the marriage by Shakespeare's alternative life in London.) Possibly the most successful marriage might have been that of Gertrude and Claudius, very evidently sexually compatible, to young Hamlet's disgust – adolescent disgust? – in the 'rank sweat of an enseamed bed'. All might have been well in Elsinore if Hamlet himself had not been so sexually confused, obsessed with Mum, and also desiring and cruelly rejecting Ophelia. One wonders if he had been as jealous of his own father previously as he now is of Uncle Claudius.

The point is that, no matter the strictures of puritanically high-minded critics who insist that the plays are 'dramatic poems' and that it is wrong to think about the characters as if they were real people, this is actually what we are likely to do when we read a Shakespeare play or see one performed. So there is nothing wrong in wondering about King Lear's wife, which is why it would be good to have Bottomley's play revived, however bad it may be. Over to the National or the RSC?

CREATIVE WRITING PROBLEMS

30 DECEMBER 2011

It came as a bit of a shock to learn from Philip Hensher's review of *Body of Work: 40 Years of Creative Writing* at UEA that there are now nearly 100 institutions of higher education in Britain offering a degree in Creative Writing. I suppose for many it's a merry-go-round. You get the degree and then you get a job teaching Creative Writing to other aspirants who get a degree and then a job teaching…and so it goes. This after all has been the way with Art Colleges for a long time. Some graduates make their living as painters, more as teachers of Art who continue to paint and occasionally to exhibit.

I sometimes think I must be one of the few surviving novelists who has neither studied nor taught Creative Writing. I was, admittedly, long ago, a writer-in residence at a couple of universities, had indeed the title of Creative Writing Fellow at one of them, but there was no Creative Writing course to teach. I was merely expected to make myself available to any students who were sufficiently interested to come and talk about writing with me, even to show me their work and invite comments. So I sat in a room and waited for callers. At Edinburgh I was fortunate to be approached by some very talented students, among them Ian Rankin, James Meek and Kathleen Jamie All the students were studying for degrees in traditional subjects: English Literature, History, Foreign Languages, Philosophy. Our meetings were enjoyable – for me anyway – but I doubt if I was of any great help to any of them. All would have become the writers they are if they had never met me. Indeed Kathleen Jamie's poetry had already won her a Gregory Award.

Hensher writes that a good Creative Writing Course can 'move a gifted but unconscious writer from the point where he says "I don't know – it just seemed to come out like that" to where he can say, "I see how I did this, and how I can do it again in different terms"'. Perhaps it can indeed do this. 'Writing, particularly of fiction, is,' as he observes, 'a matter of dense craft. Characters are structured in particular ways.'

Certainly writing fiction is a craft. You have to consider questions like the point of view – though many good novelists have always switched this as seemed convenient to them. You seek to achieve a balance between narrative, dialogue (which should also often be narrative), reflection, description, sometimes analysis. You should ask yourself questions such as 'what is the purpose of this piece of description?' or 'should this part of the novel move more quickly?' You should have read widely and considered how novelists you admire have dealt with technical problems.

Yet too much thought can damage spontaneity. Novels are made as much in the unconscious as by the conscious mind. Hensher's 'gifted but unconscious writer' who said, 'I don't know – it just seemed to come out like that' may have been wiser than his later self who understood how he did it and how he might do it again in different terms. Very often your best strokes are made without thought, and a novel may come to life when a character says or does something you didn't expect, something which therefore took you, and will take the reader, by surprise.

Reviewing the UEA book Hensher remarks on the number of graduates from the course who did well with a first book, then fell away and faded into oblivion. 'To sustain a long-term career remains a challenge for any creative programme.' This is surely an odd way of putting it, for it's impossible to see how such a programme can do more than set writers on the road. Sustaining a long-term career is their business, not their university's. All sorts of things may go wrong, in your life as well as in your art or craft. You may exhaust your material and fail to find suitable new material. You may run out of energy, or succumb to depression or alcoholism. Your publisher may lose faith in you. Your best books may fail to please readers. You may make too much money too soon, or too little ever. But it seems harsh to blame a failure to sustain a career on the inadequacies of a creative writing programme.

After half a lifetime of writing novels and after having been lucky enough to have published more than twenty, I have learned only two things: that there are certain kinds of novels I can't write, and that I really don't know any more about how to write a novel than I did when I embarked on the first one to be published. Indeed I sometimes think I know less.

POLITICIANS AND PRIVATE LIFE

23 MARCH 2012

One of the weaknesses of many political biographies is that they are so often all about politics. The authors either forget that politicians are people, and sometimes interesting people, or they assume that their private life is of neither interest nor importance. So the book becomes a record of what the politician did, rather than a picture of what the man, or indeed woman, was.

There are exceptions. One of the best of these is Roy Jenkins's biography of Asquith. Jenkins of course covers Asquith's public life in detail, acutely if at times rather indulgently. As a politician himself he is very good on the difficult matters Asquith had to deal with - notably the Irish Question, the difficulties with the House of Lords, the first two years of the Great War, and the relations between Asquith's governing Liberal party and the Conservatives. His analysis of the crisis which forced Asquith out of Downing Street is masterly.

Yet there is so much more in the book than politics, in part because politicians then were not oppressed by the demands of round-the clock news management. They had time for a life beyond politics, and Asquith, it may be said, had more time than most. He enjoyed a full social life, partly, Jenkins insists, because he was unusually capable of 'transacting his official business with great speed, but without any suggestion of neglect'. So 'he left himself plenty of time for his family and his friends, for a wider but by no means undiscriminating social life, for golf and bridge, for general reading, and for private letter writing'. Many of these private letters were to young ladies, especially Venetia Stanley, with whom he was more than a little in love.

There was a lunch-party at Downing most days of the week, with a varied, often, as he put it, 'incongruous', selection of guests. These lunches were his wife Margot's responsibility, but Asquith was usually present, and even when Margot was away, 'often went to some trouble to find guests of his own'. He would also dine out several times a month, sometimes complaining if there was no bridge after dinner. Weekends were usually spent at his house, 'The Wharf' on the Thames near Oxford. (This was before Chequers was made available to Prime Ministers.)

His reading, even as Prime Minister, was wide, and as eclectic as Margot's choice of lunch guests. In 1914 we find him reading Gosse's Ibsen, a book about spiders, Dean Stanley's *Annals of Westminster Abbey*, a history of the Wars of the Roses, 'a book by a Jew called Hirsch about the fortunes of his race in the Middle Ages', T. H. Green's *Prolegomena to Ethics*, and 'two volumes of Chamberlain's (the German) *Kant*, translated by old Redesdale who gave it to me'. He also read *Our Mutual Friend* as, Jenkins writes, 'one of a number of Dickens novels he had re-discovered that summer'. It is difficult – impossible? – to imagine Tony Blair or David Cameron enjoying such a range of reading.

Holidays were spent on a round of country-house visiting, but some of his holiday activities would cause more than a raised eyebrow now. On at least three occasions, when Winston Churchill was First Lord of the Admiralty, Asquith was his guest on a cruise in the Admiralty yacht, once boarding it in the Tay and spending four days sailing south the Chatham; another time cruising round the north of Scotland; then, more ambitiously, after travelling by train to Venice, joining it for a three-week cruise to Dalmatia, Greece, Malta and Sicily. 'It was,' Jenkins wrote, 'an almost ideal holiday for Asquith. It enabled him to play bridge at night, to read a great deal at all hours, and to indulge his taste for minute classical scholarship.' He was amused that 'Winston never set foot on shore at Syracuse, but dictated in his cabin a treatise (which I am about to read) on the world's supplies of oil'. Churchill may have been working (that day anyway), but what a hoo-ha there would be now if the Navy Minister (if we had one) commandeered the Admiralty yacht (if there was one) for a pleasure cruise in the Mediterranean, with the Prime Minister as his guest, amused to find his First Lord of the Admiralty regarding Diocletian's palace at Spoleto and declaring 'I should like to bombard the swine'. (In a footnote Jenkins asked 'but who were "the swine"?' – not however hazarding an answer.)

How curious the contrast between the leisure enjoyed by Asquith, Prime Minister of one of the Great Powers of the world, and the busy-ness today of the leaders of our greatly diminished country. They buzz about like bees. Perhaps we may wonder, as Eugene Wrayburn in *Our Mutual Friend* wondered of the bees, whether 'they overdo it'.

THE CASE FOR GUNTER GRASS

23 APRIL 2012

History is lived forwards but read backwards. We all know this, but often find it easy or convenient to forget. Criticism of Gunter Grass's poem about Israel makes the point. There were good reasons to criticise the poem's argument – that Israel as a nuclear power is the chief danger to peace in the Middle East. Yet what the critics preferred to dwell on was Grass's service as a seventeen-year-old boy in the Waffen SS, evidence surely that he has always been at heart a Nazi. The fact that he had concealed this for more than sixty years, till he admitted it in his memoir, *Peeling the Onion*, was held to aggravate the offence. That he was conscripted was generally ignored. If not ignored, then mention was made of his previous service as a Luftwaffe auxiliary, and of his attempt to volunteer for the Navy as a submariner. Looking at Nazi Germany from our perspective, it is easy – and comfortable – to be shocked.

But now is not then. Circumstances alter cases; life in Britain, indeed Europe, today is very different from life in the Third Reich. So one should try to see things as they appeared to a teenager in Danzig who, as a member of the Hitler Youth, had been, as he admits in his memoir, 'a Young Nazi…a believer to the end', one who saw his 'Fatherland threatened, surrounded by enemies'. Wouldn't it have been more remarkable if he had thought otherwise? He was a lower middle-class boy, reared on Nazi propaganda, even though he had heard his gentle and loving mother express reservations about the Fuehrer – she preferred Rudolf Hess – and say she couldn't understand 'why they've got it in for the Jews. We used to have a haberdashery sales rep by the name of Zuckermann. As nice as could be and always gave a discount'.

Maternal doubts couldn't compete with the newsreels. The young Grass was 'a pushover for the prettified black-and-white "truth" they served up' – just as British boys of his age were for our version of 'truth' served up by the BBC and British Movietone News.

In these newsreels Grass 'would see Germany surrounded by enemies, valiantly fighting what had been defensive battles abroad – on Russia's endless steppes, in the burning sands of the Libyan desert, along the protective Atlantic Wall, at the bottom of the sea – and on the home front I would see women turning out grenades, men assembling tanks, a bulwark against the Red Tide. The German folk in a life-and-death struggle; Fortress Europe standing up to Anglo-American imperialism at great cost' and every day, the long casualty lists.

How could he not believe that it was his duty to take part in that 'life-and-death' struggle – just as for instance the somewhat older man who would become the most effective denunciator of Stalinism and the Gulag fought bravely and enthusiastically in the Red Army as it laid waste East Prussia and Poland? So Solzhenitsyn must be forgiven, Grass condemned?

There was one boy who gave him pause, or, more exactly, whose memory came to disturb him and cause him to reflect. He was one of the Labour Service unit to which Grass was assigned between his time as a Luftwaffe auxiliary and his conscription into the Waffen SS. He was a beautiful blond youth – the very image of Aryan perfection – who might have modelled for any Nazi poster. He was also intelligent, industrious, helpful to his colleagues and dutiful. There was only one thing wrong with him. He wouldn't have anything to do with guns. When one was put in his hands, he let it drop. 'We don't do that,' he said, time and again. He was punished of course. To no avail: 'We don't do that.' Then the other members of the troop were punished, on his account. No good: 'We don't do that.' So, resentful and angry, they took it out on him. They beat him; one boy pissed on his bed. But still, 'We don't do that,' he said, refusing the gun. Eventually he was taken away. Someone said he was a 'Jehovah's Witness' – whatever that was. They had no doubt as to his destination.

A nasty story. 'Typical young Nazi thugs' may be your response to the way Grass and his mates treated the boy they had come to call 'Wedontdothat'. But I wonder: might he not have been given as hard a time by his mates in a British barracks? How would a boy who proclaimed himself a pacifist and conscientious objector have been treated in one of our tougher public schools at any stage of the war?

Grass himself was 'if not glad, at least relieved' when the boy disappeared. 'The storm of doubts about everything I had had rock-solid faith in died down, and the resulting calm in my head prevented any other thought from taking wing; mindlessness had filled the space. I was pleased with myself and sated.'

Years later he took 'Wedontdothat' as the model for a character in his novella *Cat and Mouse* – 'marvellous, off-beat character – fatherless altar boy, student, master diver, Knight's Cross recipient, and deserter' – and had him drop his weapon 'slowly, deliberately, the better to ingrain it in our memory'.

Then came Grass's attachment as a Panzer gunner in a unit of the Waffen SS. He can remember neither shock nor horror, 'I did not find the double rune on the collar repellent.' Instead he 'probably viewed the Waffen SS as an elite unit that was sent into action whenever a breach in the front line had to be stopped'.

Appalling? Yes, if you read history backwards. But at the time, this was surely a natural response. It would have been natural to feel pride – no matter how that pride was mixed with fear. The Fatherland in danger? Wasn't assignment to a crack unit even something to be welcomed?

Of course it didn't turn out like that. This was the winter of 1944. Everything was beginning to fall apart. 'Soon I witnessed an event that should have made the downfall of the German Reich evident – the organised chaos of defeat moving slowly, then with dispatch, and finally at breakneck speed.' But they went on fighting, even when there was no hope of victory, little even of survival. They went on fighting because there seemed to be no alternative – on what was left of the Eastern Front anyway.

Terrible months for everyone, but he came through eventually to be compelled to accept that: 'I had been incorporated into a system that had planned, organised, and carried out the extermination of millions of people. Even if I could not be accused of active complicity' – in that extermination – 'there remains to this day a residue that is all too commonly called joint responsibility…What I accepted with the stupid pride of youth' – his membership of the Waffen SS – 'I wanted to conceal after the war out of a recurrent sense of shame.'

It's easy to blame his membership of the Waffen SS, easy so long as you refuse to try to imagine yourself as a German boy in 1944; easy also to condemn his decades of silence on the subject, if you make no effort to understand the depth of the shame he felt.

IN PRAISE OF
THE LITERARY JOURNALIST
14 JUNE 2012

With few exceptions literary journalists moulder in the grave, and
are soon forgotten. They may get some sort of posthumous life
if they are made the subject of other books. John Gross rescued
a few from oblivion in *The Rise and Fall of the Man of Letters*.
Otherwise it is usually only those who were also poets, novelists or
social commentators such as Matthew Arnold, who are not soon
forgotten. When I was young the Sundays were dominated by
Connolly, Mortimer, Toynbee, Nicolson, Davenport. I delighted
in them all, and equally in V. S. Pritchett in *The New Statesman*.
All of course were excoriated by F. R. Leavis in stern puritanical
Cambridge. Fair enough: to academics engaged in 'close reading'
or, later, in 'theory', the literary journalist has always been a *flâneur*
or dilettante. Nevertheless all those I have mentioned wrote well,
and were influential in their day. Pritchett was of course a master
of the short story and so his work survives. But the others? 'Where
are the snows of yesteryear?'

Desmond McCarthy belonged to an earlier generation. Born
in 1877, he died in 1952, just about when I was starting to read
the Sundays and the weeklies. He had been a distinguished theatre
critic as well as a reviewer and literary journalist, this last the term
he applied to himself. There can't be many left who read him
regularly. It was a surprise to come the other day on a collection of
his pieces published in 1984 – I suppose I reviewed it somewhere.
The surprise was only slightly diminished when I saw the first
chapter was a memoir of McCarthy by Lord David Cecil, whom I

knew to be his son-in-law. So I suppose Cecil persuaded someone at Constable to publish the book. I can't believe it was a profitable venture.

Nevertheless it was worth publishing and most of the essays remain enjoyable to read, and are sometimes illuminating. McCarthy had the happy gift of the striking phrase: the characteristic of Henry James's later style 'is a spontaneous complexity'. This seems to me exactly right.

On the other hand, though McCarthy took great pleasure in James's novels, his criticism of James's theory 'that it was necessary to get rid of the omniscient narrator' seems very much to the point. James saddled novelists with the tyranny of 'the point of view', his insistence 'that everything recounted in a novel should be seen through the eyes of some character in it; not necessarily the same, and perhaps through one character after another'. There's a lot to be said for the theory, which subsequently attracted Conrad and Ford Madox Ford, and I remember being reproved by an editor who criticised the first chapters of a novel I had sent her because the point of view kept shifting. She may have been right in this case – the novel anyway was later abandoned. Yet McCarthy remarked on 'the fatal flaw' in the theory. 'If the narrator is abolished' – that is the omniscient author as narrator – then 'the characters who narrate in his place become inevitably endowed with the novelist's own peculiar faculties and intellectual temper.'

'Inevitably' is probably an exaggeration. Good authors are often capable of impersonating a narrator very different from themselves. Yet McCarthy is surely justified in observing that this is what happened in James's later novels: 'The characters were often so steeped in the colours of their creator's mind, that their individual tints barely showed through the permeating dye.' This is not the sort of language that academic critics may use, but it is surely an acute observation. Seeing everything through the eyes of one character may actually deprive that character of the individuality he or she should have.

The collection includes a nice essay on 'Reviewers and Professors'. It is written as a dialogue between a literary editor and an aspiring young reviewer. 'It is useless,' the editor says, 'your coming here and telling me you can review five-sixths of the books that come out.' Instead the young reviewer should make it clear that he knows a lot about a few subjects, and branch out from there. 'You are enthusiastically and ignorantly interested in literature. Your enthusiasm is to the good; your ignorance to the bad. But that can be overcome – if you condescend to crib from critics who know much more than you do. If you are going to be a literary reviewer, you must start by acquiring a Library of Criticism. You must lay down the Professors.'

Good advice, then and now. The best literary journalists write from a well-stored mind. Some of them may even be worth reading, in small doses anyway, long after they are dead. Desmond McCarthy proves to be – somewhat to my surprise.

THANKS

To Mark Amory, Clare Asquith and *The Spectator*.

David Elliott, Gavin James Bower and Beatrice Watson at Quartet.

MORE FROM THE AUTHOR

Praise for **Death in Bordeaux**, a taut and psychological thriller set between the corridors of Vichy power and the backstreets of Bordeaux – and the first in a trilogy of crime novels that follow the charismatic detective Lannes through the events of World War II:

'[Readers] will be delighted to learn that this stylish, atmospheric, satisfying policier is the first of three to feature Superintendent Lannes'

Boyd Tonkin, *Independent*

'Thought-provoking, fast-paced and gripping throughout, it is the work of a natural storyteller at the height of his powers'

David Robinson, *The Scotsman*

'...in pacing, telling and intent, this is a cut above your usual crime novel'

Rosemary Goring, *Herald Scotland*

'The novel's ending is wonderfully unorthodox – and grimly convincing'

Andrew Taylor, *The Spectator*

'I think **Death in Bordeaux** is both a thriller and a "literary" novel: a difficult trick, but in my book the greatest to bring off. I look forward eagerly to volume two'

Robert Harris

In 2012 Quartet Books published the second in Allan Massie's brilliantly-reviewed crime trilogy, **Dark Summer in Bordeaux**. With his son's safe return, Superintendent Lannes and his wife can, at last, have some joy amid the grim reality of Vichy France. Not that the unexplained murders seem to have stopped...

'Massie's evocation of France on the brink of the invasion is vivid and convincing, and this fine novel, set in a period of moral turmoil, introduces a humane and memorable detective'

Joan Smith, *Sunday Times*

'Remarkable'

Jessica Mann, *The Literary Review*

The third in the trilogy is coming soon...

WWW.QUARTETBOOKS.CO.UK